Praise

Dr. Matthew X. Joseph provides a powerful journey for every educator into the realm of self-reflection. Brilliant insight into the direct links between creating community, the power of connections, and strong individual leadership.

Jennifer Ingold
Grade 8 Social Studies Teacher
@msjingold

Stronger Together is an essential toolkit of battle-tested tools & strategies that will elevate any administrator's game. As a 20+ year veteran, I kept finding myself air high-fiving Dr. Joseph because he is spot on so many of these insights on how to shape school culture so every student wins. This guide is helpful no matter if you are a new school leader, change of career administrator, or a veteran who happens to find yourself in a new school community.

Craig Martin, M.Ed.
Superintendent
@craigcmartin12

Stronger Together

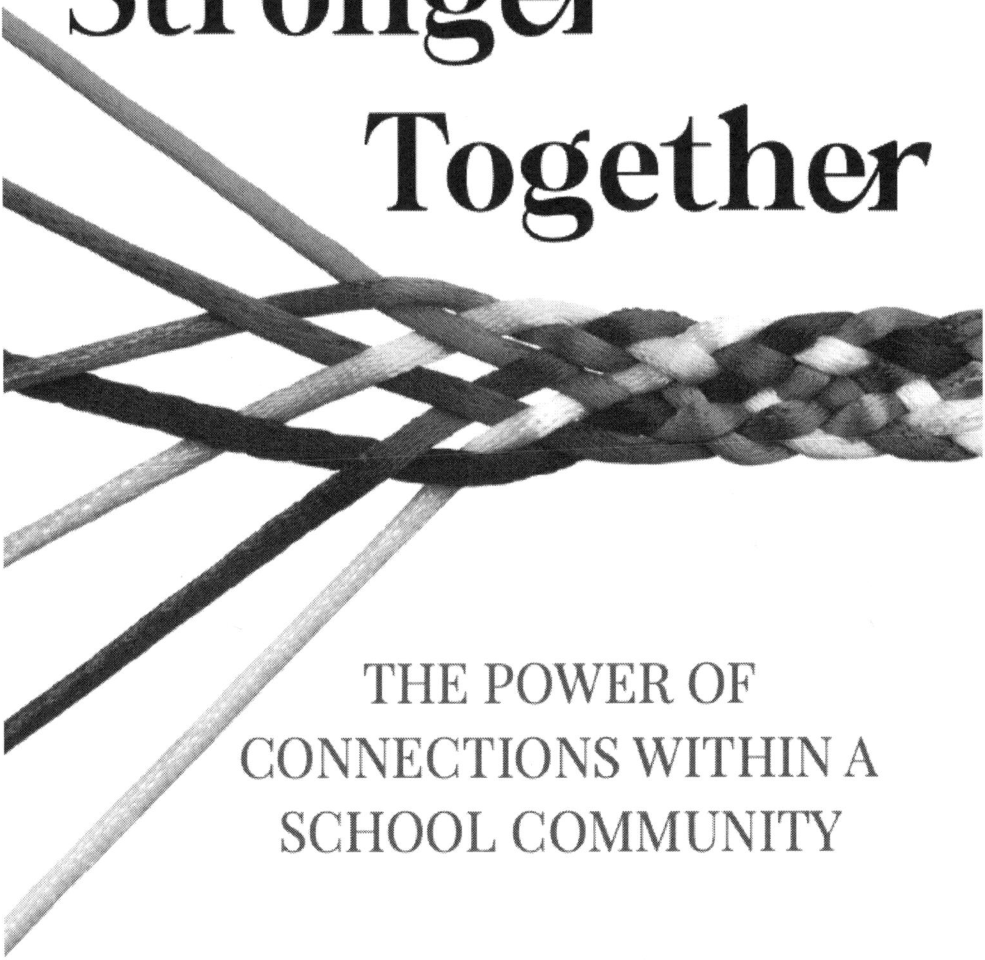

THE POWER OF CONNECTIONS WITHIN A SCHOOL COMMUNITY

Dr. Matthew X. Joseph

First edition 2021

XFACTOR

https://xfactoredu.org

X-Factor EDU

Our Mission Statement:

Be Unapologetically
YOU

Thank you to all our X-Factor partners!
Your efforts will directly support educators' growth and access to resources necessary for improving teaching and learning.
Because of you, we are all Stronger Together.

CODE BREAKER INC.

Breaking code isn't just about programming, it's about disrupting the status quo. It is about challenging social norms. It is about having critical conversations. It is about challenging systematic beliefs. It is about educating the whole child - mind, body, and soul.

To learn more about

CODE BREAKER INC.

and our services,

visit www.codebreakeredu.com

INSPIRE · INNOVATE

LEAD · TEACH · LEARN

Code BREAKER

Shout out

So, if X-Factor EDU is about being Unapologetically You, then I want to do a "Shout Out" more than acknowledgment or other formal start to books. Just feel more like me.

This entire book is about how working together makes us more energetic, more active, more effective, and work is just a more fun place to be. Stronger Together is not just a book title to me; it is my professional way of life. From the first day I stepped on Springfield College campus and joined my New Student Orientation group (Shout out NSO), my first day as a teacher in an open classroom, and every day I drive to work or speak at an event, I believe collaboration makes be better. This book and X-Factor EDU would never be more than an idea without collaboration.

I met Brian Aspinall CEO of Code Breaker Inc. exactly one year ago, December 2020. We clicked and kicked around ideas for my next project. I quickly signed on as a Code Breaker Inc. author and began writing Power Of Connections. I also worked closely with Daphne McMenemy, the Managing Director at Code Breaker Inc., as she had the challenge of editing my book. Ya, my random flow of ideas is always a challenge to edit.

After publication, I began organizing and facilitating the Code Breaker Innovators Lounge and collaborating more with Brian and Daphne. Besides being two awesome people, they are visionaries, and I learned a ton from collaborating with them.

In the summer of 2021, Brian approached me to add a publishing arm to X-Factor EDU and be a publishing affiliate of Code Breaker Inc. I was honored! So, in August 2021, X-Factor EDU publishing was launched. Brain encouraged me to write the first book for X-Factor EDU, so I jumped right back into writing.

So my book started to take shape. And again, Stronger Together partnership was the foundation to bringing my ideas to life. I needed an editor. Code Breaker Inc. best-selling author Christine Ravesi-Weinstein just completed her book, *Fighting Your Inner Voice,* and wanted to take on a new challenge. So I asked about editing. She saw this as a new challenge and jumped in. Be careful what you wish for, Christine. Little did she know the first project would be, well, a challenge. Oh, not because of her BECAUSE it was my book. I like to speak my books and have the "notes app" type, or I often write with no punctuation, or I randomly brainstorm and put it in writing. So being the editor of my book is one hell of a challenge, BUT she took it on and turned strings of words and ideas into a book. Her talent and efforts are impressive, and I am grateful for the care she put into my book.

THANK YOU Brian, Daphne, and Christine. You really showed what it means to be Stronger Together.

And note neither Daphne nor Christine edited this Shout Out, so any errors are not on them :)

Table of Contents

Foreword

By Brian Aspinall

CEO Code Breaker Inc.

Best Selling Author of Code Breaker, Block Breaker, Risk taker, and When Passion Meets Project

We used to attend school because that is where the knowledge was. School, by definition, was a physical structure of bricks and mortar often filled with inspirational messages in the form of commercial print.

"Hang in there!" says the upside down cat.

School, by definition, was a place that sorted kids based on age and abilities based on one or two subject areas.

Shit. Wait a second. Let me try that again.

School, by definition, is still a physical structure of bricks and mortar often filled with inspirational messages in the form of commercial print.

School, by definition, is still a place that sorts kids based on age and abilities based on one or two subject areas.

Yet, the ways in which people engage, collaborate, and learn has changed very drastically in a short period of time. Teachers are Tik Toking their way through lessons, encouraging students to take risks, talking about mental health issues, political protests, armed intruders, celebrity gossip, etc.

In the same physical location. And that is okay.

There is a push to knock down physical walls and completely change physical school settings rather than innovate inside the box. That box though, that physical school building, has tremendous potential to become the greatest incubator of brilliant ideas. As long as we allow it.

Quite often, school is built on a foundation of compliance. But with compliance, we limit creativity. Rules are typically meant to govern human behavior and keep people safe. However, perhaps our best lesson is to teach students to question all rules. Not to be defiant, just to make people think. To make people grow. To make people better.

Industry has changed, especially coming out of a pandemic. Virtual workspaces are here to stay, offering a reduction in traffic emissions. What if schools followed suit? What if the definition of school still includes physical spaces, but instead, students attend as necessary? Radical thought perhaps, but that is because it has never been done before. Herein lies the problem.

"We've always done it this way!"

But this way doesn't work anymore. If given the opportunity to skip school, would your students come to class? Why or why not?

What if students went to science class to learn about molecules because they needed to know important pieces of molecular information rather than attending science class because a timetable schedule demands it.

What if we also redefined community? I'm involved in a plethora of digital communities with people I've never met in person but who I hold in incredibly high regard, including the author of this book. People who are experts in their own right. People I can count on as needed and when needed, not because it is 9:30a.m. on a Monday.

We live in a world of on demand, easy access, and constant bombardment of advertisements, political agendas, and celebrity gossip. It is imperative we teach our young people how to filter -- and not just clean water -- the internet. And that may, or may not, require students to be in the same physical space at the same time, sorted by age.

We have a tremendous opportunity to make drastic, radical, and much needed change. Not necessarily to the physical components of school, but those systems in which we cannot see. Evaluation systems, for starters, don't celebrate failure. They punish it. They sort kids based on the results of scheduled events. We can no longer preach embracing failure while working in a system in which failure is punished.

In a world that changes overnight, the only strategy guaranteed to fail is not trying something new. So develop your safety net in the form of quality connections with ego-free relationships. Find those people who make you better. People who make you smarter. People who make you stronger. Find your synergy.

They may exist in your physical school building.

Or they may not.

And that is what makes teaching and learning today so fucking special.

#StrongerTogether Kick-Off

By Dennis Griffin Jr,

Warren Buffett stated,
"Culture eats strategy for breakfast!"

Even with Warren Buffett's sought-after and respected mind, we still emphasize creating the best strategies for success. Since we have yet to heed Buffett's words, I believe it is time to alter this phrase. Culture does not eat strategy for breakfast; CULTURE IS BREAKFAST!!! That is correct. CULTURE IS BREAKFAST! Do you know what the number one component of culture is? If you do not let me tell you, it is you and me, your family, friends, co-workers, students, and members of your community. In short, CULTURE is about PEOPLE's connection to remove them from the isolated fate and constraints in a results-driven world. Strategies and strategic plans often bring out the best part of a plan, but not always the best out of a person or members of your team. This has been a conundrum that

I have seen many individuals struggle with for years. The bottom line is that your superior strategy is nothing without people who believe in the vision and are willing to go through the trials and tribulations to make that vision a reality. The strategy does not allow us to deter because we are so dedicated to the strategy. Strategy created blame when a goal that was derived from the strategy was not successful. Strategy isolates individuals until they are permitted to shine. People want to shine all the time. People want to be part of something greater than themselves. People want to cheer, but they also want to be cheered on.

One of the shocking narratives in our society is that we ultimately associate culture with sports organizations. We applaud the effectiveness of winning organizations that state that their culture is the importance of their success. We revere these organizations that we even elevate some to the level of being called a dynasty. It appears as if any individual that joins that organization is an instant success. They change the way that they walk, the way they talk. They change the way they perceive and believe in themselves and the people they are mutually responsible for. Witnesses marvel to such a degree that they often think that if they execute the same play or had a particular player, they believe their organization will be just as successful as the dynasty. Strategy is often a short-term fix to a complex problem. Far too often, the strategy may have materialized from one individual that had the opportunity to cultivate others; however, what happens when that individual goes away? Here is where we get it wrong. We look for sustainability within One member of the organization when we should be in pursuit of evolution. #StrongerTogether is about creating a culture whose synergy ensures that we are no longer living or operating in silos in the quest of supporting one another to become the best version of ourselves. #StrongerTogether comes at a price. You will have to be able to sustain the dissonance of your challenged and evolving paradigms. You must be willing to reflect. You must be vulnerable enough to acknowledge what you do not know. You must openly share your values and seek alignment with the values of others.

#StrongerTogether is the embodiment of nothing great that was ever accomplished in isolation. Now more than ever, with our world's state, we need individuals who are willing to go beyond the theoretical narratives of creating a change in our world to bring change. But, unfortunately, no matter how strong they are, they will not be able to do it alone. #StrongerTogether is about ensuring that we are willing to learn so that we advocate and hear those that might be deemed voiceless. #StrongerTogether is looking the current reality in the eye and then walking side by side with one another, knowing that we matter. #StrongerTogether is the determination to make a difference. The difference that we will make is initiated by touching a heart that transforms our individualistic values into a collective ideology that powers our minds.

Welcome to #StrongerTogether. You have a unique gift that has been waiting to be tapped into. You might have been afraid to take this road for many reasons, but here is the one thing I am willing to declare; #StrongerTogether is not about the authors of this book; it is not about the words on the pages. #StrongerTogether is a revolutionary movement that will unite a society of learners to change the needs of our world. I can declare this because I have witnessed several thought leaders present in this book that has pushed me to new heights and refused to let me not tap into my unique gift that will serve as a conduit of change.

Culture is our breakfast, and the only way to make that happen is to eat with those that will make us #StrongerTogether.

Introduction
Power of Us

I've learned that people will forget what you said, people will forget what you did, but people will never forget how you made them feel.

–Maya Angelou, American Poet

In Power of Connections: Connecting Educators, Cultivating Professional Learning Networks, & Redefining Educator Collaboration, from Code Breaker Inc., I wrote, stressed, and shared how lifelong learning requires effort. In 35,000 words I showed how collaboration, as a learning method, has been the fabric of adult learning. I focused on global professional learning networks (PLNs) and highlighted how our ability to connect with today's technology is limitless. I truly believe a PLN is a mindset, not a one-shot association. These connections help educators be innovative in their classrooms, schools, and beyond. Ultimately when managed well, innovation can improve student outcomes. Power of Connections, was a book about taking your global professional relationships to the next level.

Now, I want to build off the global collaborations I talked about in Power of Connections and focus inward on our own school buildings. Collaboration in a school building is essential to building a stronger community.

Seven years ago I wrote my dissertation at Boston College. It focused on building a collaborative, healthy culture in schools. One big finding from the study was:

When staff, teachers, and parents work together, schools can be happier, healthier places. In schools where shared goals are created, everyone feels like they belong to something bigger than just their classroom.

Hence #StrongerTogether.

I've had the pleasure of being a school and district leader in various capacities throughout my 27 years in public education. Roles such as the Director of Curriculum and Instruction, Director of Digital Learning and Innovation, elementary school principal, classroom teacher, and district professional development specialist have shown me the positive experiences collaborative opportunities can have on a school. On the other hand, they've also shown me the damage that working in silos can have on school culture.

In collaborative schools, educators and staff work together toward common goals. Educators assume the responsibility of every student's success. In a "silo" school, every person works for themselves. Adults blame parents and administrators for student failure. There are many good teachers working in "silo" schools, and many are open to collaboration. We must find a way to tap into that.

So what's the difference between collaborative schools and "silo" schools? The answer is school culture. Staff working in schools with collaborative school cultures function differently from those which depend on administrations to define working conditions. In collaborative cultures, staff practice creative leadership together and take responsibility for helping all students learn.

The success, or failure, of any school improvement, depends upon staff behavior. When good teachers work together, they support one another's journey toward better instruction. Leaders who need to raise student achievement are too often driving with the brakes on. Collaborative cultures take the brakes off and accelerate a faculty's capacity to improve instruction. If the brakes are ever going to be removed, educational leaders must build cultural norms that support staff working together.

Let's highlight some of the differences between collaborative cultures and "silo" cultures. First, in collaborative cultures, educators:

- Support one another's efforts to improve instruction.
- Take responsibility for solving any and all problems.
- Accept the consequences of their decisions.
- Share ideas.
- Are energized by the ideas of their colleagues.

In "silo" cultures, educators:

- Discourage challenges to the status quo.
- Depend on school administrators to solve problems.
- Blame others for their difficulties.
- Complain about the consequences of decisions.
- Limit expansion by claiming ownership of their own ideas and individual projects.

As educators, we have to find ways to publicize ongoing collaborative work; acknowledging those who have taken on new roles and risks in their schools. Then, as projects or ideas take flight, we can focus on the ways to showcase the collaboration that enhanced the work, the school, and thus, the community. Finally, we can use these celebrations to recruit new co-workers and encourage future collaboration. In this way, collaboration becomes rooted in the school's culture. This book will dive into ways educators can do this; be Stronger Together

As a principal, I personally saw the positive effects of the Stronger Together mindset on the collaboration and culture of my school. I launched many collaborative initiatives: a teacher-leadership team, teacher presentations at state and national conferences, stakeholders' voices in school-budget initiatives and policies, and a new mission. One impactful activity in particular, was a full day of team-building activities. Can you guess when that took place?

If you said the first PD day of the year, you're right! The staff didn't need to listen to me blab about information they could read in an email. They needed to connect, collaborate and learn to trust each other. We went to the local YMCA and participated in a ropes course to build teamwork and collaboration. I'm sure some of you are saying, "That's not professional development." While some are thinking, "I wish we did that."

Think about it this way: Did we learn and develop the following skills by doing the ropes course?

- Communication
- Conflict Management
- Support
- Listening
- Trust
- Respect
- Shared Credit

Of course we did! Those skills are part of a collaborative community and accountability to others. Does it matter how or where those skills were learned? No. The goal was for our staff to learn them. The YMCA was simply a fun way to do so.

In addition to focusing on ways in which educators can establish a collaborative school culture in their buildings, I also want to give each of you a chance to absorb the book and provide time to think and plan next steps. In order to accomplish this, there will be "pause moments" at the end of each chapter. As educators, we are constantly observing, analyzing, and deciding how to (or not to) implement new learning into our own practice. At the end of each chapter, there will be guiding questions to help turn thinking into action. As educators, we are always growing, learning, and improving, but a danger in our profession is getting too comfortable with past strategies and methods. Educational settings and tools are constantly evolving and we must do the same. We have to challenge ourselves and be willing to examine and modify our approach if we're going to be successful in educating students. We cannot be stagnant. We must be a "living Google document," constantly tweaking, refining, updating, evaluating, and taking in feedback.

Being Stronger Together is a journey that starts with one step. Let's take that step and open the doors to collaboration and a growth mindset. Let's be Stronger Together.

Chapter 1
The Why

Alone we can do so little; together we can do so much.

—Helen Keller, American Author and Disability Rights Advocate

Author and inspirational speaker Simon Sinek said: "Start with why." As I begin this journey, I'll follow Sinek's advice and start with why creating collaborative school communities is not just a need—but a must—for us to continue to grow as learners and leaders. As educators, we have two responsibilities for all our students:

- Create a safe physical and emotional learning environment.
- Provide the best education possible.

The foundation of both responsibilities lies in educator collaboration. Sounds simple in theory, I know. But in practice, it's far more complex.

Unlike professionals who work in the private sector, teachers spend most of their days with other people. While I understand a majority of that time is in front of students teaching, we need to find new ways for educators to collaborate when they are not with students. I get it, it can be hard to find three minutes to even use the bathroom, but creating collaborative opportunities are a must if we are going to reduce the feelings of isolation that working in silos can create.

In the teaching profession, we use the word "silo" to refer to the environment that's created when teachers walk into their classrooms, close their doors, and simply teach. Teaching in a silo can become isolating; you experience little to no interaction with colleagues. This lack of interaction can stunt professional growth and become a detriment to student learning. In my experience as a teacher and school/district leader, I have observed teachers getting territorial over classroom space, subject-area content, and supplies and resources. Some teachers prefer to work unsupervised and uninterrupted. This singular mindset creates the silos and isolation that sometimes breeds an intimidating culture in schools. I have seen teachers benefit and grow from sharing and learning with each other. Think about what we tell our students to do when they have a question: "Ask three before me" or "Work with a partner." As leaders, we need to empower and encourage our staff to do the same. Teachers and administrators, do you collaborate when you have a question?

Isolation can be detrimental to one's professional development. By interacting with our colleagues, we can gain new insights. We can also share ideas and experiences that will improve our teaching.

Remember, at the end of each chapter, I am asking you to pause and reflect on the content you've read. Maybe take notes in the book, or a journal, or in any way that suits your style. Self-reflection is a critical tool for our own growth.

Pause Moment

Reflect on the following questions?

- How many colleagues do you interact with each day/week?
- How many hours per week do you spend engaged in dialogue with your colleagues?
- How many hours do you spend working alone?
- How often do you eat lunch with a colleague?
- How often do you co-plan, co-teach, or facilitate a joint lesson with another teacher?

Chapter 2
Common Language

If everyone is moving forward together, then success takes care of itself.

—Henry Ford, American Industrialist and Businessman

Chapter 1 focused on the necessity of "why" you are doing something. As we start to dive into highlighting culture as a critical aspect of a school community, we have to articulate why establishing a collaborative culture is essential. Part of having the ability to communicate the why of a collaborative culture is understanding what school culture is.

I hear leaders using culture and climate interchangeably as it relates to schools. Although these two terms have similar meanings, they express two different concepts.

Think about this.... An educator brings cupcakes in on Monday and puts them in the conference room with a note, "Have a great start to your week!" Everyone is happy. It's a nice surprise, puts you in a good mood to start your Monday, and let's face it, who doesn't love a free treat?! The following Monday, the educator does it again; another great start to the week. Bringing cupcakes in every Monday morning is an example of impacting climate. The current temperature in the building is cheerful and happy. This small act can turn a bad day into a good day or make coming back from a weekend a little easier. This is the basis of the school climate: creating a mood (hopefully positive).

Climate can change quickly, and not always for the better. What if that teacher doesn't bring cupcakes in on the third Monday? Do teachers say, "Hey, no cupcakes?" Or, "I was really looking forward to a treat today; Monday's stink!" With one simple act, you can change the climate.

Culture, on the other hand, would be an email going out after that first Monday saying, "Thank you to Ms. Smith for the treats; it was so thoughtful of you! Next week, I'll get them. Who's next?"

Perhaps this is too simplistic an example. But culture is something that is built and then carried on; it cannot be changed quickly.

Based on my research, I would define school climate as the collective mood, or morale, of a group of people. Climate describes the shared perceptions of the people in a group or organization at a specific time. Culture includes how people feel about the organization and the beliefs, values, and assumptions that provide the identity and set the standards of behavior.

My research findings directly connected a positive culture to higher job satisfaction, and increased instruction. Unfortunately, some leaders don't distinguish between climate and culture and therefore, don't make use of the most effective strategies for creating a positive school culture. Instead, they try to improve the climate by relying on extrinsic rewards: preferred or duty-free lunch, an ideal parking spot, or cupcakes, for example. Bringing cupcakes after a weekend may help a few teachers come in on Mondays, but this will not impact the culture of the building long term.

I think of climate as "how are we feeling around here" versus culture as "the way we do things around here." It may feel like a semantic argument, but the culture of the school is the personality of the building rather than the current mood or attitude. Both climate and culture impact the people's behaviors in the school, but the climate is more narrow view of the functioning of the institution. Culture digs deeper considering what people believe in and value. Culture is a by-product of the historical working relationships in a school. Climate is a function of how current staff perceives current working relationships.

While different from culture, a positive climate is still essential in a school; it's the primary leverage point for any culture. If school leaders want to shape a new culture, they must start with an assessment of climate. If the culture is ineffective, climate issues were probably to blame. They likely were problematic before they became rooted in the culture.

A school staff develops a common culture to pass on to the next generation of teachers. New teachers arrive yearly with their own ideas about how to teach. Through their college classes and practicums, teachers are immersed in theories of best practices and current methodologies. If the culture of their first job does not embrace these new ideas, the new teachers will quickly learn that to fit in, they will need to conform. Because new teachers want to fit in and feel like veteran teachers, they are vulnerable to the school's culture, one which they had no influence in building.

As we move along in our journey together, we will dive into how we examine a school's culture and begin to move toward a collaborative, healthy school where ideas flourish and staff and students are proud to be part of the community. How do you want staff and students to feel when they enter school every morning? Are teachers dreading coming to work in the morning? Do students walk into the building with their heads down, trying not to interact with others? Or, are teachers inspired; beginning each class with energy and positivity for their students? Do you hear laughter in the halls when students arrive? Having a positive school culture impacts not just the attitudes of the students and teachers, but the entire learning experience.

How influential is school culture? Well, the dominant atmosphere in your school will affect everything that goes on inside its walls. This goes beyond the student body: it also involves how teachers interact with each other, their students, and the parents.

A toxic school culture is a place where staff are highly divided. The purpose of assisting students has been put second to the goal of serving the adults. Negative values and selfishness are prevalent. A toxic culture is not a suitable environment for any school. On the other hand, positive school culture is where your efforts are seen as positive experiences for both students and staff. Success, joy, and accomplishment are all the main features of positive school culture. When your school has a positive culture, teachers are excited to come to work because they see the big picture, and students are better for it; intellectually and emotionally.

Pause Moment

Reflect on the following question: "What are the foundations of my school's climate and culture?"

A few thoughts to assist with this reflection:

- Do I see positive teacher-student interactions?
- Are there collaborative relationships between the school leader and faculty?
- Are there collaborative relationships between faculty members?
- Do our goals focus on learning and include high expectations for student achievement?
- Are students feeling safe, connected, and engaged?
- Do we have policies promoting social, emotional, ethical, and intellectual skills?
- Are there clear, appropriate, and consistent expectations and consequences to address disruptive student behaviors?
- Does our school have a high level of parent involvement?

Chapter 3
The Problem with Silos

No matter how brilliant your mind or strategy, if you're playing a solo game, you'll always lose out to a team.

–Reid Hoffman, American Entrepreneur, Venture Capitalist and Author

Working in silos limits the collective thinking that's critical to innovative ideas needed to transform teaching and learning. Change is complicated, and uncomfortable, and as such, schools are sometimes unwilling to do so. There can be many factors at play: existing high achievement, possible union pushback, consistent turnover, etc. However, moving outside of our comfort zones and into the learning zone is a step towards breaking school silos down. With skilled educators and the digital resources of today, we have ideas and strategies available 24/7. We have the power to shift a school into a collaborative community and to have critical conversations about exciting and innovative change in schools.

Think about it: Do you establish a culture of shared purpose and continuous improvement?

I didn't introduce that reflection question with any qualifiers like "in your classroom" or "in your school." That's because when we talk about collaborative communities, we talk about all the areas and stakeholders of a school.

- Classrooms
- Schools
- Families
- Central office
- School committee

You can walk into a school and know instantly whether or not you want to be there. A collaborative culture is more than merely attending a scheduled meeting, or sharing lessons as part of common planning time. It requires transparency, honesty, integrity, dependability, accountability, and commitment to shared goals. A collaborative culture is a mindset that must be fostered by leadership. Johnson and Papay (2012) found that it was not the working conditions "such as well-maintained facilities or access to modern technology" (p. 2), but rather the positive social conditions such as collegial collaboration that were a predictive factor in influencing teacher job satisfaction. Flores (2004) further identifies that school workplace conditions directly impact overall teacher development and learning. Collaboration is a mitigating condition for teachers to grow in the profession and accept and implement change effectively. Collaborative workplace relationships and cultures are associated with a supportive environment and better development opportunities for teachers. When school leaders support collaboration by seeking out teacher input in decision making, offer sufficient teacher support, and create a community that fosters collaboration, teachers are more prone to remain in those schools.

A collaborative community presents opportunities for shared leadership, educator ownership, and sharing of instructional and pedagogical ideas. We have the power to shift a community into a collaborative environment and have critical conversations about innovative change in schools and instruction.

When educators work together, we create a better learning experience. It may seem obvious, but brainstorming is not possible without collaboration. Educator collaboration provides security and helps jump-start the generation of ideas that may seem crazy at first.

Working with a small group of trusted teachers allows a "silly idea" to become a creative lesson plan. Likewise, peer-to-peer collaboration can turn a small idea into the seeds for something fabulous.

When we work together, we create invaluable learning experiences. Teacher collaboration positively impacts student achievement because more ideas are infused into lessons and allow us to explore new territory.

Teachers are specialists in their classroom design and planning. However, research shows that even seasoned teachers benefit from sharing ideas. Teachers can discuss different strategies and offer samples from their own experiences. When schools encourage teachers to collaborate and share ideas, teachers contribute to each other's toolbox of best practices. This process increases a teacher's contribution to overall school improvement and positive culture.

Teacher collaboration happens when educators work together to increase student achievement. If our purpose as educators is to positively influence student achievement, then teacher collaboration is our journey. Collaboration is not a duty to complete, or a box to check off; it's a continuous method that is improved by social networks and access to new technology.

Another advantage to moving out of silos and tapping into different perspectives and ideas is shared responsibility for students' learning. The more people invested in a student's education, the better the student's chances to be successful. You've all heard the saying, "It takes a village"? Well this is what collaborative cultures support; the idea that all teachers are responsible for the success of all students.

But even with all the obvious benefits, active collaboration among educators is still not happening in any formalized or common way. Perhaps this is because some educators are unaware of the benefits of the collaboration process.

Here are a few benefits I have seen the collaboration process have on the positive tone of a building and the success of it's students.

- When teachers come together to share information, resources, ideas, and expertise, learning becomes more accessible and effective for students. Since teachers who collaborate on

instruction are all on the same page, the level of academic rigor rises.
- Teachers understand and talk about the relevant data from both formative and summative assessments. Collaborating around data gives a sense of shared responsibility for celebrating success and analyzing failure.
- When teachers interact and share ideas, they share instructional strategy collections that support creative instruction and lesson plans.

The move from silos to collaborative cultures needs to be genuine. Teachers cannot simply "go through the motions" as a means to be in compliance with school and/or district initiatives. Rather, they need to believe in the strategies, ideas, and testimonials that show the importance of moving out of our silos and into collaborative cultures.

Pause Moment

Reflect on the following questions: Are there collaborative relationships between faculty members in my school/district? What can I do to increase and/or strengthen those relationships?

Chapter 4
Leadership is Action

A leader takes people where they want to go. A great leader takes people where they don't necessarily want to go, but ought to be.

–Rosalynn Carter, Former First Lady and Mental Health Advocate

While "the boss," or principal, may be the one who leads a school's initiatives, any staff member or student can demonstrate leadership as a means to enhance learning. As Donald McGannon said, "leadership is action, not position." School leadership, which is the process of enlisting and guiding the talents and energies of teachers, students, and families toward achieving common educational goals, is not exclusively for administrators. As a building and district leader, I have seen that staff and students can be leaders too. When we talk about "collaborative leadership" or "positive leadership," we're not talking just about the school principal or superintendent, but about all educators. WE ARE ALL LEADERS. You are never *just* a teacher or staff member; you are a leader because of your actions.

Leading by Action

People follow people, not positions. They respect people who have accomplished something worthwhile and demonstrated that they deserve to be followed. Leaders need to modify practices and change mindsets. They can't just talk about it; they must take action. What follows are the actions taken by effective leaders to empower all students and educators.

Action: Have Vision

Amidst all of the current information, media sources, data, improvement plans, and initiatives vying for our attention, and dollars, it can be hard to focus on one overarching goal. However, having vision gives us direction. Vision is a mental picture of the future that guides us, motivates us to grow and improve, and gives us a sense of purpose. In leadership positions, vision helps us focus on the unchanging goal in an ever-changing environment. Having an instruction vision will turn lessons into units and units into a scope of big-picture learning for students. A vision helps to communicate goals and focuses our work on what is essential for student success. We will dive deeper into vision and mission planning in schools in a later chapter.

Action: Make a Difference

More often than not, it's a teacher who inspires a student to become a lifelong learner. Making a difference is not about *what* we do, but rather *how* we do it. By being both respectful and relevant, leaders inspire colleagues and students to become confident and motivated critical thinkers and learners. When caring for students and collaborating with fellow staff members, leaders must be willing and able to use the most current and efficient learning tools and methods to create an environment conducive to learning.

Action: Add Value

Adding value is about opening doors to better opportunities for students and colleagues. Unfortunately, many leaders are too quick to take charge. But influential leaders listen to understand those who they lead. A good leader listens to what every person believes is important and takes the needs of their students and colleagues into account when making decisions.

Action: Listening

We can always learn from those around us. Effective listening gives us knowledge and perspectives that increase our leadership capacity. Being open to feedback and new ideas helps us learn and grow. Listening to someone shows you care about what they're saying and you value them as a contributor to the community. Giving value to others creates a work environment built on trust. Having trust in the building/district develops a sense of togetherness.

Action: Take Risks

Anything worth doing involves risk. While it can be scary to try new things, it's a lot easier when someone else jumps in first. So JUMP into something new and exciting. Successful leaders, guided by vision, are calculated risk-takers. They're willing to try something new, even if they fail. So rather than focusing on the numbers and what they've already accomplished, influential leaders reflect on the *how* and *why* of what will make their vision a reality.

Talent wins games, but teamwork and intelligence win championships.
– Michael Jordan

Schools are experiencing a dramatic shift in how they're run and structured. As school and classroom leaders navigate this changing landscape, they need to establish direction, influence others, and initiate sustainable change. Such leadership requires a dynamic combination of mindset, behaviors, and skills to enhance school culture through collaboration and teamwork. As previously stated, a leader can be anyone who has the vision to make a difference and the courage to make that vision a reality.

Now that it is clear that anyone in the school, by way of their actions, can be a leader, it's time to dive into creating that collaboration together. Cultivating a culture of collaboration requires structure, protocols, and routines. Collaborative leadership is a style that recognizes the importance of interpersonal relationships and cross-functional collaboration.

Collaborative leadership is the presence of opportunities for shared leadership, educator ownership, and the sharing of instructional and pedagogical ideas. Collaboration is a talent and skill developed through humility, patience, and vision. This can happen in a district, a school, and a classroom. Just as it is important to have action to establish collaborative leadership, it's important to have structure to sustain a collaborative culture. Here are some of the steps necessary to move a school or classroom to a collaborative-leadership model:

Establish group/classroom goals and norms: To have the highest quality interactions, you must have a safe environment. This initial step involves individual accountability combined with group outcomes. It keeps the group on task and sets a purpose. For example, group goals and norms might be:

We commit to...

- consistent, positive, and timely communication with one another.
- regular reflection on our own and each other's productivity and well-being.
- finishing each meeting with action items and deadlines for future work.
- being responsible, accountable and direct.
- being a critical friend and accepting a critical friend.
- having fun.

Use discussion and dialogue: We must remember to "use our words," just like we ask of our students. For example, your collaborative team may need to select a new curriculum, analyze data, or study new instructional methods. A discussion enhances a conversation and allows group members to state their thoughts or ideas before a consensus is reached or decisions are made. Moving from discussion to dialogue enables the team to broaden individual knowledge, incorporate multiple perspectives, listen actively, and stay focused.

Working through conflict is also essential with discussion and dialogue. With an increase in collaboration, there may also be an increase in conflict. Furthermore, opening up dialogues may lead to conflicts, so having strategies for your leadership team to monitor conflict will support individuals in the most critical moments. This step takes professional judgment and trust, but often provides the most important growth opportunities for your team.

Develop problem-solving and decision-making strategies: It's not up to the leader to make decisions and then communicate those to the group. That is the opposite of collaborative leadership. Instead, the team's responsibility is to consider the issues, decide the direction, and then count on the leader for support. Problem-solving and decision-making strategies may vary in different settings, but having a consistent plan to move forward, solve problems, and support decisions is a staple of collaborative leadership.

Assure all voices are heard: This may seem like an obvious statement when discussing collaborative leadership, but knowing and doing are two different things. Being heard is more than allowing participants to speak in meetings. A collaborative leader must facilitate participation from all members and welcome the input of new participants. Seeking the opinions of others builds trust and inclusiveness from the start. Trust is the belief or confidence that the leaders are reliable and have the school's best interest at heart. It is the glue that holds together collaborative leadership.

Ask, "What if?": Moving from the problem-solving stage to a solution requires one last conversation about the unknown consequences of a decision. Preparing for the unknown will assist a team with supporting the conclusions. If possible, you should have multiple voices available to lead the discussion around the "why" of a decision. As we all know, there will always be people who push back on collaborative leadership decisions. Vetting the "what ifs" will build cohesiveness in a group.

Henry Ford once said, "Coming together is a beginning, staying together is progress, and working together is a success." I believe these actions and steps will assist in building a collaborative culture that will have a lasting positive effect on your school and district.

Pause Moment

Reflect on the following questions: What are some of the leadership traits you possess? How do you use those traits to support a collaborative classroom/school?

Chapter 5
Setting the Table

We don't have to do all of it alone, we were never meant to.

–Brené Brown, American Professor

When "collaboration" is discussed in schools, it is not always welcomed with open arms. Educators who have had success working individually may feel like they're being infringed upon; their space is being invaded. However, when a school community respects each other and acknowledges individual skills and participation, all staff can move forward in a positive environment. In addition, effective collaboration provides teachers opportunities for improved practices and a feeling of being valued in a school environment. Known educational author on teacher effectiveness, Harry K. Wong, said "the trademark of effective schools is a culture where all teachers take responsibility for the learning of all students." The key to strong collaboration is educators recognizing that a single student isn't the responsibility of only one teacher, but everyone; all teachers, leaders, and staff.

One common theme in all of the interviews and site visits conducted on school culture was: A collaborative community has the potential to improve teacher performance, as well as student performance.

In all of the reading I've done on school culture, never did I read about a magic potion or buzzword to solve all of a school's problems. However, one idea seemed to weave into every recommendation and success story - **collaboration**.

When a school community has been created that respects all stakeholders and acknowledges individual skills and participation, everyone can move forward in an environment built on positivity. The more effective a teacher becomes, the more students will reap the benefit.

As I reflected on the positive impact of collaborative communities on my school, I struggled with how best to support leaders, teachers, and learners. I read an article by Carrie Leana on school reform. She studied over 1,000 4th and 5th-grade teachers and concluded that collaboration was a key to achievement. She went on to say that students showed higher gains in math when teachers collaborated on lessons. This trusting community led to closeness and, in turn, student achievement. I have seen this same success in the multiple school districts in which I have worked.

A school with a collaborative culture improves the professional capacity of all individuals in the school:

Staff: When two or more educators collaborate, they create a product for students made up of each of their best ideas. This makes for a better lesson, more effective teaching practices and greater buy-in.

Administrators: Collaboration between district and school leadership fosters a community of stakeholders (teachers, parents, students, and community members) who see the effectiveness of collaboration.

Students: An effective learning community allows students to reach out to solve problems and share knowledge. This skill builds collaboration and encourages/supports more profound learning and skill retention.

Families: When a school has a strong home-school relationship, it lends itself to open communication, support, and a network of people focused on student learning and high academic achievement.

In general, collaboration supports students, staff, and administrators by:

- Developing higher-level thinking skills.
- Encouraging and sharing strategies for student-faculty interaction and familiarity.
- Building self-confidence.
- Enhancing learning experiences.
- Increasing oral and social communication skills.
- Creating a community of active and creative learning.
- Using a team approach to solving problems.
- Fostering an atmosphere of cooperation and accountability.

Educator collaboration cannot just be the informal conversations we have in the parking lots, hallways, or at the lunch tables. These discussions are less about collaboration and more about making small talk, or, in many cases, commiserating together. A professional collaborative culture requires teachers and leaders to share, support and explore new ideas together in a formal setting. The benefits of developing a collaborative community will reduce teacher attrition, improve student learning, and create the type of school that everyone searches for when they decide to become an educator.

But a positive culture doesn't just happen. If we are setting the table for this shift, the school leader must "walk the talk."

When administrators maintain a sense of optimism, their teams act with more confidence and collaborate more effectively. Leaders and districts need to create positive work environments in today's fast-paced, rapidly changing educational institutions. Although this is challenging for every leader, it's critical to navigate these uncharted waters with care. Positive leadership is not a topic of conversation just because of recent hardships in the profession. However, the shifts we all face due to the recent pandemic do remind us just how important positive leadership strategies are.

As a leader, you directly influence the behaviors of others. Parker Palmer, an author, educator, and activist who focuses on issues in education, community, leadership, spirituality, and social change, said, "Relational trust is built on movements of the human heart, such as empathy, commitment, compassion, patience, and positivity." When coupled with schools' current needs to face change and new possibilities, being a positive educational leader is paramount.

Positive leadership makes a difference in productivity, satisfaction, and happiness at work. Leading with positivity also helps to build trust among colleagues, and it becomes safer to open up to change.

Shifting from the distractions of constraints and toxic culture empowers people to be their best. Positive leadership supports staff to focus on their own growth and potential. It sounds simple, but it's harder to do. Positive leadership requires embracing positive possibilities and dealing with the criticism that goes along with it. It requires leaders to look for potential—even in situations, or people, they usually can't find anything in which to celebrate. Being a positive leader does not require an increase in budget or a change in school plans. Instead, it requires courage to cultivate a team's well-being.

Pause Moment:

Reflect on the following questions: Do I welcome new ideas? What can I do to increase and/or strengthen ideas focused on collaboration?

Chapter 6
Self-Reflection

Without reflection, we go blindly on our way, creating more unintended consequences, and failing to achieve anything useful.

—Margaret J. Wheatley, American Writer

So now that we know we *need* to make the shift to collaborative leadership in our schools, the question becomes *how* do we do this? We must start by reflecting on our current school community. Brené Brown said, "Imperfections are not inadequacies; they are reminders that we're all in this together." One of my favorite movies, *The Greatest Showman*, is known for its show stopping number, "This Is Me" by Keala Settle. This song is undeniably empowering when it comes to reflecting on yourself. You can listen to it here:

One practice I did not use early enough in my career as a principal was self-reflection. That said, now I use it regularly and find great benefits from it. Reflection takes many forms, and is an integral part of our own education and growth. In fact, if you practice it often enough, self-reflection can become a skill. Great leaders and teachers reflect on their practice and tweak their plans, units, interactions, and attitudes regularly. In a profession as challenging as teaching, self-reflection offers leaders an opportunity to constantly get better and grow with the changing climate.

Self-reflection is about asking yourself thought-provoking questions so you can develop a deeper understanding of your current thinking, performance, and needs. New thoughts lead to new emotions and consequently to new actions and personal growth. Too often in education, we are so busy that we aren't even aware of how we're feeling; we usually don't make the time to take a breath. Taking that breath can rejuvenate us and get us excited for new challenges. These "breaks" are when we can take time to self-reflect. I recommend these strategies to support your reflection:

Look in the mirror: The first step with any self-reflection is to consider looking in the mirror and being honest with yourself. Before looking deep, you should examine your beliefs, successes and areas of improvement. Like anything, we can't improve and grow if we don't first admit to where we are starting.

If you do what you've always done, you'll get what you've always gotten: Educator and counselor Jessie Potter used this expression in 1981. It is unavoidable, we all get comfortable with doing the same things. As educational settings evolve and change, however, we must be willing to update and modify our approaches to educating students. As uncomfortable as change can be, we must reflect on our current practices and see if it's what's best for students. Ways we can evolve to ensure we are growing and reflecting include:

- *Recording a lesson.* Recording a lesson and watching it back, allows educators to assess their own practices. Consider watching the lesson with a colleague or coach in order to start a discourse about your practice.

- *Making a portfolio.* A portfolio encourages educators to combine the various elements of their teaching into a cohesive digital "binder" or storyboard. A portfolio typically starts with a teaching philosophy or statement, before moving into lesson plans, assignments, work samples from students, and evaluations from colleagues. Though less focused on classroom practices, a portfolio is an opportunity to reflect on teaching overall.

- *Engaging in a teaching peer review.* Peer review is a collaborative approach to self-reflecting. Teachers can ask a trusted colleague to observe their classroom and give them feedback on their teaching. Colleagues can agree on an observation protocol or a list of effective teaching principles to focus on during the lesson.

Write while you reflect: I am not someone who likes writing, but recently I've found this reflective practice to be insightful; it provides critical insights and allows for free-flowing thinking that I can look back on over time. Additionally, putting it down on "paper" holds you accountable to your own admissions. If you don't commit to changing what you've committed to understanding yourself, you're not being true to who you are.

Enlist a critical friend: I can be biased toward my strengths and weaknesses, and because of this, I must consult with a critical friend if I am going to truly commit to self-reflection. The best thing about using a trusted colleague is they will give you honest advice and feedback that provides insight into who you are as an educator.

As classroom or building leaders, you shouldn't just focus on self-reflection, you should also reflect on the culture you've created in your classrooms and/or buildings. In all the buildings and districts I've worked, I've prioritized ensuring collaboration is high and builds a healthy school culture. Putting strategies in place to build culture requires reflection. When a school develops a healthy culture, it encourages all stakeholders to work together.

Once we reflect, we need to create goals for not only ourselves, but the school as well. Reflection paired with setting goals will give you a long-term vision and short-term motivation. In addition, goal setting focuses our learning and assists us in organizing time and resources to achieve goals efficiently.

Set Goals: By setting high, clearly defined goals, you can measure and take pride in the process of achieving them. Seeing forward progress helps motivate us even when the going gets tough. Seeing the small wins as you work toward your goals will give you more self-confidence to achieve great things.

Below are some key steps to take when writing goals:

- **Reflect:** The only way we can reasonably decide what we want in the future and how we'll get there, is to know where we are *right now* in our current level of practice.

- **Identify your dreams and turn them into goals:** In hindsight, we often say, "I wish I did that," but why not do it NOW? *Think about what thrills you as a teacher/leader.* Write down all your dreams. Don't think of any dream as too far-fetched. What is the classroom you dream of teaching in? Who is the teacher you dream to be? Dreams are not just the result of wishful thinking; they are the core for developing pathways and thinking tactics (strategic planning). Dreams are the beliefs that things can get better and are the foundation upon which motivation is built. Your dreams will turn into motivation and then action when you define your goals.

- **Make your goals S.M.A.R.T.:** I first learned about S.M.A.R.T. goals when I started my role as a principal and began evaluating teachers. S.M.A.R.T. goals were developed by George Doran, Arthur Miller and James Cunningham in their 1981 article "There's a S.M.A.R.T. way to write management goals and objectives." Yes that was over 40 years ago, but we still use the reference today. The acronym S.M.A.R.T. means Specific, Measurable,

Attainable, Realistic, and Time-sensitive. This is not a new idea I have developed. S.M.A.R.T. goals have been used in many districts across the country. Let's dive deeper into the background of this idea:

- *Specific:* Goals should be explicitly written and clearly define what you are going to do. Specific is the What, Why, and How of the S.M.A.R.T. goal.

- *Measurable:* Goals should be quantitative, so that you have tangible evidence/data supporting whether or not you have accomplished it. Qualitative or subjective goals don't help schools, or you, make forward progress.

- *Attainable:* Goals should be achievable; they should stretch you slightly so you feel challenged, but within reason. You can meet almost any goal when you plan your steps wisely and establish a timeline. But it is unlikely you will accomplish a goal you set at 100%.

- *Results-focused:* Goals should measure outcomes, not activities.

- *Time-sensitive:* Goals should have a timeframe; one year, two years, or more.

Here are some questions to consider to help organize your thinking around your own S.M.A.R.T. goals. I developed these over years of creating S.M.A.R.T. goals with teachers and trying to push them out of their comfort zones.

- **Specific:** What will the goal accomplish? How will it be accomplished and why should it be accomplished?

- **Measurable:** How will you specifically know whether the goal has been reached? What number are you striving for?

- **Attainable:** Is the goal possible? Do you have the necessary knowledge, skills, abilities, and resources to accomplish the goal, and still be challenged?

- **Results-focused:** What numerical outcome are you looking for with the goal?

- **Time-bound:** When do you hope to accomplish the goal?

Once you know what your goal is, begin to build action steps. When you document and track progress, you hold yourself accountable through reflection. A goal without action steps is like a gym membership you don't use: nice to have but not worth anything. The process of achieving a goal must include accountability. I recommend having a critical friend to hold you accountable. When you share your goals, you're more motivated to reach them.

Engaging in reflective practices allows educators to dedicate time to evaluating their teaching, examining their curricular decisions, analyzing student feedback, and making updates to improve student learning. Educators who take time to reflect on what went well and what missed the mark can better assess areas for improvement and make necessary modifications. Developing a reflective practice needs to be deliberate. Using these reflective practices will help keep you engaged and present in your own growth. Balancing a reflective mindset with actionable improvements will help you stay on a path for continuous improvement.

Pause Moment:

Take some time to use the learned strategies for writing S.M.A.R.T. goals to draft your own along with the action steps needed to turn your dreams into a reality.

Chapter 7
Have the Vision to be Collaborative

Vision is the art of seeing what is invisible to others.

—Jonathan Swift, Anglo-Irish Satirist, Essayist, and Political Pamphleteer

One must start with a clear vision and a sense of purpose to develop a collaborative community. I touched on this as in Chapter 4, but as you set out to build collaborative cultures of your own, I want to dig deeper into the idea. Influential leaders, no matter what the profession, can vividly describe their vision and paint a clear picture of their destination. They build teams and define the steps to get there. It is critical to know where you are going before you can ever take that first step.

Vision refers to having a mental picture of the future that guides, motivates growth, and gives a sense of purpose. In education, vision helps us focus on our unchanging goals in an ever-changing environment. Leaders prepare for the instructional future by looking at how students will learn best as technology and needs change. Educators have the vision to plan lessons, create a classroom environment conducive for learning, and ensure students are always safe.

A vision, regardless of context, always includes a mental image or picture, a future orientation, and a direction or goal. Too often, vision is used because it's a buzzword, rather than something an educator actually believes in. True vision, however, provides a roadmap for the school and all its stakeholders. Once established, educators can communicate this vision to inspire, motivate, and engage students.

Think of a Royal Caribbean cruise ship. What is the first step when some CEO says, "I want to invest in starting a cruise line?" The first step better be bringing in someone to design the boat before the first part is ordered. Stephen R. Covey, author of *The 7 Habits of Highly Effective People*, said, "Begin with the end in mind." Without knowing your goal, purpose, and direction, how do you think you are going to get there? Having a vision will inspire, motivate, and engage people as you begin developing a collaborative community.

In July of 2013, I walked onto the campus of Boston College to start my doctoral program. I was nervous; I knew only one other person. I sat and looked around. I thought, *"What did I get myself into? Can I do this?"* On the first day, we were given a card to stay focused on our goal. The card read "Plan with the end in mind." I kept it on my car's dashboard to remind me, everyday, of my journey and goal.

Sure, vision provides a picture of the future, but more importantly, it inspires people to take initiative. A clear vision also assists if, and when, you go astray along the way.

When a school leader, classroom teacher, or district administrator believes in a vision, others will see it in their actions, mannerisms, motivation, and passion. You hear a lot of people say: "I'll believe it when I see it." Think of vision as the reverse of that statement. If you believe in your vision and model it every day, others will "see it." They will see the vision and be clear on the direction.

Moving from Vision to Mission

Vision and mission statements provide schools with an overview of where they want to go and what they want to be. Vision statements establish clear expectations and standards for the whole school community and help the school reach common goals. If moving to a collaborative culture is the vision, now it's time to act.

A mission statement provides an overview of the steps necessary to achieve that future vision. A mission is longer and is the "how-to" statement that helps schools achieve their vision. If you're ready to define a vision for collaboration, and create a mission statement to get there, here are a few steps to turn your idea into action:

- Identify a vision and mission team. Ensure at least one representative from each grade level, department, and all other programs are represented (e.g. counselors, Special Education, English Language Learner teacher, parents).

- If the school already has an existing vision and mission statement, bring those to the table when (re)creating the school-wide vision and mission. You have to know where you've been before you can decide where you need to go.

- Develop a plan to include all staff in the process of providing and collecting feedback for the revision of the vision and mission statements.

- Mission and vision design teams should review school data that identifies areas in need of improvement. The data might include: demographic data, attendance data, student achievement data, etc.

Questions the mission and vision design teams must focus on:

- What kind of school do we desire to be?
- What should be highlighted in our vision statement?
- What do we need to do differently to achieve this vision and make it a reality?
- How do we stand out from other schools?
- What unique opportunities do we have at our school?

The design team will need to regroup to reflect and discuss before anything is implemented. This meeting will be a time to brainstorm and listen to feedback as a team. When all feedback has been discussed, and all voices heard, the team should discuss it together. A draft vision and mission statement can only be written, once feedback is considered. This can be a long process, but it's a valuable process, and not just if you're looking to shift to a collaborative culture. Vision and mission are important because culture is about "how we do things." If it's not represented in the vision of the school, collaboration will be seen as just an initiative, rather than a culture.

Pause Moment:

Reflect on the following questions: Do we have a vision in our school? Do our actions represent that vision?

Chapter 8: Recognizing Roadblocks

The road to success is paved with doubters and haters.
–Matshona Dhliwayo, Philosopher, Entrepreneur, and Author

While effective collaboration provides teachers opportunities for improved practices and produces a feeling of value in a school environment, it is not always welcomed with open arms. Harry K. Wong, an author on teacher effectiveness, said, "The trademark of effective schools is a culture where all teachers take responsibility for the learning of all students." The key to solid collaboration is when educators recognize that a student shouldn't be the responsibility of only one teacher, but all teachers, leaders, and staff. This shift in thinking will open the door for collaboration in schools. When pushback occurs, leaders must step up and continue to invest in their vision and drive towards collaboration. The following are potential roadblocks and push back you might experience when trying to implement effective collaboration.

Forced collaboration: As educational leaders encourage more collaboration among teachers, leaders must genuinely lead the way and model the collaboration they want to see. An authoritarian or "I'm the boss" leadership style leads to decreased collaboration and negative feelings over time. Remember, leadership is action, not position. Just because you told teachers they have to collaborate, does not mean you will get the collaboration you seek. Any ask a leader makes before building the why and vision of such a request will increase feelings of marginalization and lead to increased cynicism in the process.

To lead our schools to a place that supports and encourages all 21st-century learners, leaders must build a foundation for collaboration. If we show respect in the process and acknowledge our staff's unique contributions to the community, we can quickly move schools forward in a positive collaborative environment where everyone is a teacher and a learner.

A decision is already made: To build a collaborative culture, leaders must move past just identifying problems and start relentlessly pursuing solutions. Collaborative schools are action-oriented. They eliminate outside factors and don't use them as excuses for not changing behavior. But when it comes to actively seeking solutions, leaders cannot ask to collaborate on input *after* a decision has been made. Staff will feel insulted and immediately push back on collaboration. Collaborative schools embrace an honest evaluation of their current state. They examine every action and contest behaviors that are not in line with their vision. Honesty builds trust, which is an essential element of all collaboration. The ability to build trust is an important strategy when building a positive collaborative community.

Any time there are collaborative decisions to be made, an individual's needs can cause disagreement among the group. Typically, when one person or a group attempts to impress their ways upon others, stress and displeasure set in. Misuse of positional power is unnecessary because, in most situations, all parties can reach a shared understanding and/or solution to a problem. When the school community sees you constantly working to find collaborative solutions, they will be more understanding when you must make swift, executive decisions without asking for input. This could be the case in a discipline matter or a time-sensitive budget need. In a collaborative community, teachers, students, administrators, and families are all on the same team working toward the same goals. If leaders are building a foundation of collaboration, they must model this collaboration in as many decisions as possible.

Inequality: All individuals working in schools, whether in a leadership position or a classroom role, should be striving for equality all the time. It is rare that you will find a situation in which everyone gets exactly what they want, however, the goal in developing a collaborative school is to find a solution that is *acceptable* to everyone involved. As all math teachers will tell you, it is a rarity that there's only one solution to a problem.

A simple way to start forming a collaborative school culture is by including teachers in what are typically administrative decisions. When possible, provide more open-ended activities and/or agendas at meetings that require staff to problem-solve and draw on a range of skills. For example, see if they have a solution for an unpopular duty or a schedule with choppy breaks. When we think of providing meaningful experiences in education, we tend to think of the students. But to be equitable in our leadership, we can't forget about the teachers too. To lead a collaborative school, one needs to promote initiatives and a vision that shows appreciation for *all* staff and creates a connection beyond just the school environment.

No time: To be a leader who promotes collaboration, you must schedule time and opportunities for educators. If you do not make time, you will get pushback from staff because, let's face it, there's never enough time.

Take this scenario for example: teachers meet in groups to discuss and edit lesson plans. This time allows educators to share successes and challenges in a safe and supportive environment. Teachers can study lessons together and make changes based on the group's experiences. Teachers then test the newly adapted lesson with their students and report back to the group with the results. This creates a reflective process of building and evaluating lessons. If teachers find that process questions overwhelm students, the group can modify the activity instructions to focus on the subject matter itself.

These collaborative practices (and many others) cannot happen without leaders providing a clear and defined schedule of time to do so. A leader can be creative with schedules or duties to find the time, but regardless, leaders who practice and design efficiency in collaboration will find they increase staff involvement and productivity, and reduce pushback. Educators will feel less stressed out not having to find or schedule their own time to collaborate. Be creative with collaborative time both inside and outside of school. Take a few minutes before or after school to check in with staff or colleagues. Never forget about collaborating virtually using Google Docs, Zoom, or email. If time or location is an issue, digital tools are a good resource.

One of the biggest roadblocks I have seen in creating collaborative schools is **TIME**. I urge you to make time to collaborate. In a world where there never seems to be enough of it, we must make the most of it when we find it. Too often, I hear, "I would love to be a part of that, but I don't have time." The term *time management* is a misnomer. You cannot manage time; it's not possible. However, you *can* manage the events and tasks in your professional lives so as to squeeze the most you can out of the time you have. We would all love more time, but we only get 24 hours, 1,440 minutes, or 86,400 seconds each day (cue the *Rent* theme). How you choose to use that time depends on the skills you've learned through self-analysis, planning, evaluation, and self-control. Much like money, time is both valuable and limited, and it must be protected.

A school day is constantly go-go-go. As it already is, most leaders put in a couple of hours before and/or after students and staff are in the building to tackle the email, phone calls, and paperwork they can't get to during the school day. Unfortunately, change isn't going to decrease the demands on our leaders' time. Change means stress, and, as a result, educators may want nothing to do with it. School leaders must expect a certain degree of pushback with collaboration. Whether this pushback derails a school's efforts depends on the leadership team's skills in supporting the desired shift. I believe the schools that successfully create a collaborative environment have leaders who model the actions needed to build a strong foundation. Because of the time shortage, educators and leaders can quickly put these strategies into place and eliminate roadblocks.

Clarity in your mission: What does your school/ classroom stand for? What are your core beliefs? Effective leaders can vividly describe their future vision and can paint a clear picture of that destination. Communicate your vision in newsletters, in the staff room, and in your actions.

Reach out to staff and stakeholders, part 1: One of the best ways to connect and create authentic bonds is to reach out to people just because. Spend a day writing a friendly note and drop it in staff mailboxes, or deliver it in person. Consider calling home to share positive news about a student rather than something negative. The positive connections you make will breed collaboration down the line.

Reach out to staff and stakeholders, part 2: After initial communication, leaders' next steps will be to check in regularly with teachers and staff to see how everything is going. Consider holding individual meetings with teachers who may initially be resistant to collaboration. Developing personal relationships with staff and making them feel comfortable when voicing concerns or discussing classroom challenges, reinforces the very foundation of a collaborative culture.

Visit classrooms: Collaboration increases when staff feel their leader is visible. School-wide collaboration is based on the pulse of a building or district. For school leaders to be visible and have the knowledge of instructional practices being used in their school(s) to deliver growth-providing feedback, they will need multiple methods of classroom visits. Observing the dynamics of all relationships in the building, teacher-to-students, student-to-student, and teacher-to-teacher, will foster trust with the staff.

Have lunch with students: When staff observe their leader out of the office connecting with kids, they will be more open to collaboration. Leaders are modeling collaborative thinking and reinforcing the message that this work isn't about them, but rather the community in which they work.

A collaborative community is an opportunity for shared leadership, educator ownership, and improved instruction and pedagogy. And while it's necessary to anticipate potential roadblocks, it's also important to learn about and be able to identify false collaborative communities.

In negative school communities, staff may be afraid to offer suggestions or ideas because they fear being criticized. As a result they are likely to retreat to their own silos. The negative environment is perpetuated because new staff who bring hope, energy, and ideas are quickly oppressed by the culture. Sadly, new teachers won't just retreat to their silos and keep to themselves, they will also succumb to the negative ways of thinking that are entrenched in the negative school community. This, ultimately, continues the cycle of negativity. As you build your tool box to increase positivity, eliminate negativity and work towards a community of togetherness, try a few of the following recommendations:

Be a part of the solution: Make sure you are not the one being negative. Have you seen the movie *Rounders*? It's based on the card game Poker. Matt Damon's character Mike McDermott says, "If you can't spot the sucker in your first half-hour at the poker table, then you *are* the sucker." If you hear your principal or other teachers saying, "It is really negative around here," and you don't spot it... well maybe reflect on that for a day or two.

Spread positive messages: Highlight positive people, activities, and ideas you see in the school. Leave a note on a teacher's desk or in the staffroom about a great thing, act, or teaching strategy. You may be the only one spotting great things, but a positive school culture has to start somewhere, and once you do so, it will become contagious. Speak up.

Have the courage to step up: Sometimes, it takes a teacher confronting negativity with a conversation to start a movement towards positive school culture. If someone is typically negative or a roadblock to change, ask them why. Yes, this may be awkward or difficult, but a simple conversation can go a long way. Too often in schools you hear a lot of unhealthy talking or complaining i.e., parking lot conversations. Someone having the courage to call it out, even gently, can be the step needed for others to see their bad habit.

Collaboration can start with just one person: Be that one. People have an affinity for those in their teaching circles or content areas. Typically these people are in close proximity to them; often right next door. Make it a goal to broaden your circle. Take a walk down the hall. Swing into classrooms to say, "Hi," ask the teacher a question or open a discussion about their likes, dislikes, or challenges outside of school. This information will assist you in remembering and acknowledging small, seemingly trivial things to engage in conversation about next time; kids' names, birthdays, etc. Consider seeking out someone new to sit with, or volunteer for a committee at your next staff meeting. Knowing details about others goes a long way in relationship reciprocity and building a community that's Stronger Together.

Visit someone else's space or building: This is one of my favorite ways to collaborate. Most teachers, and many principals, are unaware of what goes on in a colleague's classroom because they've never seen it. Think about how informative it is for elementary principals and teachers to view the environment of the schools to which students matriculate. I know it can be hard to not feel like you're being judged or evaluated when an administrator or evaluator comes to your building/classroom, but positive school cultures assume positive intent. While this is just a suggestion right now, it will be revisited later for practicality, depth, and structure in order to get it off the ground.

No educator or staff member wants to work in a toxic school. It takes leadership from teachers and administrators, time, and direction to rebuild and change these kinds of communities. I believe that most schools are not entirely negative, but it is hard to let go of negativity, especially if it has festered over time. The key is to start with ourselves and make the courageous and conscientious choice everyday to not add to the existing negativity. I know this can be difficult, but with vision and confidence, you can stay the course.

Pause Moment:

Reflect on the following questions?

- Am I visible and present in the school? What can I do to increase and/or strengthen my own visibility?
- Do I empower and motivate others? How can I do more to motivate and inspire others?
- How often do I reach out to parents to share a positive message?
- Do I contribute positively to my learning community? What can I do to increase positivity with colleagues?

Chapter 9: Harnessing a Stronger Together Mindset

Teamwork is the ability to work together toward a common vision.

—Andrew Carnegie, Scottish-American Industrialist

When you spend time at a school where people seem focused, enthused, and energetic, you start to understand the importance of a positive, productive organizational culture. Unfortunately, not every school culture is developed to the point where staff and students enjoy being there (Hodges, 2018). Tim Hodges, Ph.D., is the Senior Consultant at Gallup and shared that in 2019 U.S. students in grades five through 12 found that 29% considered themselves not engaged. The research he did found the result similar among school staff. Hodges shared that 51% of fifth- through eighth-grade school employees were also not engaged at work.

So how do we solve this? What's the answer? First, school administrators and teachers must take a hard look at their school cultures and form plans to build environments designed to generate more enthusiasm, school pride, and overall productivity. The good news? This starts with a mindset, and when we work together, we form a team approach and shared accountability.

Those who've been successful in this endeavor have found the results to be a win-win for everyone. And in many cases, everyone in a school community sees the need for a better culture — they just don't know how to make it happen.

Successful schools generate and maintain a sense of teamwork, shared goals, and productivity that ease the minds of students and staff. Of course, problems still exist in these schools, but there's a strong sense of optimism and hope for the future. So what makes this mindset?

In Power of Connections: Connecting Educators, Cultivating Professional Learning Networks, & Redefining Educator Collaboration, I wrote about the POWER you have when developing your global Professional Learning Network (PLN). POWER is an acronym that represents the five foundational traits I look for in a PLN. They are:

P: Purposeful
O: Opportunity
W: Win-Win Situation
E: Engage
R: Risk-taking

Power of Connections focused on why these were critical when forming global PLNs. When it comes to forming collaborative bonds in your school, you also have to have a POWERful foundation. Without a POWERful foundation, initiatives will crumble, and the naysayers will have a larger influence. I want to expand on the POWER acronym of global PLNs and share how the same concepts can make the culture within a school strong and long-lasting.

Sometimes, what holds colleagues or schools back from collaboration is knowing where to begin. Having a clearly stated understanding of what individuals want to achieve, will make your connections Purposeful. Communicating the purpose will excite new ideas and create more lasting momentum towards initiatives.

Professional styles, practices, and routines are delicate topics for many educators because they can become deeply personal. Those who work in isolation can find it difficult to share ideas or have their practices discussed. This can lead to conflict within a collaborative team. To move the collaboration forward and not have any defensive or overloaded staff, you must have realistic expectations and ensure purpose.

If the purpose of the collaboration is not clearly communicated, understood, and collectively owned, cooperation may be off on the wrong foot before it even begins. Having a purpose builds buy-in from the staff and the community. Some questions I ask myself before a collaborative initiative are:

- Why is it important for us to collaborate? Will it enhance our idea/work?
- What will success look like?
- What will our team get out of this activity?

Collaborating without a purpose can cause more issues than not collaborating at all. Too often, we plan a staff meeting and give a task such as "work together to brainstorm a new dismissal process or tech purchase." It is critical to make collaborative time purposeful by focusing on real instructional supports and ideas. Instead of having a general collaborative activity, have a structured, coordinated PD/activity/meeting plan, and give advance notice, so staff can come prepared. Plan an activity to enhance instructional practices like examining student work together to calibrate scoring.

The importance of continuous growth and learning for adults in schools has been well documented. Unfortunately, professional development and collaboration are usually a "one-size-fits-all" experience. When collaboration is purposeful for teachers and allows for opportunities to choose their own learning, it will contribute to building a culture of growth-mindset. Creating the conditions for teachers to collaborate, and collaborate well, is a crucial factor for greater student learning and achievement (Darling-Hammond, 2000).

Any staff member or student can demonstrate leadership to enhance learning as long as they are given the Opportunity. School leadership, which is the process of enlisting and guiding the talents and energies of teachers, students, and families toward achieving common educational goals, is not exclusively for administrators. With the new paradigm shift in education focusing on collaborative practices and critical thinking, all staff and students can, and should, develop a collaborative community.

As I wrote earlier, people follow people, not positions. They respect people who have accomplished something worthwhile and demonstrate that they deserve to be followed. My friend, and Boston College classmate, wrote about the positive effect of distributed leadership in schools. Distributed leadership describes practices that allow for multiple individuals to be leaders in an organization (Morris, 2016). A primary focus of distributed leadership is the interactions between the individuals in leadership roles. He found that teachers who were involved in leadership activities had a greater degree of job satisfaction. This points to the power of collaboration. If all teachers were given opportunities to lead, they would feel more connected to, and a part of, the school community.

Having opportunities to collaborate or socialize with peers is critical to developing this community. While some teachers may be willing to participate as is, it's important to make sure your community is not exclusive; the same few teachers are always facilitating, participating or leading school endeavors. The more opportunities provided to staff the more inclusive the school community will become.

There's not many things worse for school morale than leaders or educators who practice the "Do as I say, not as I do" philosophy. When this happens, you can almost see the loss of enthusiasm and trust among the staff. This philosophy breeds cynicism and disappointment, two mentalities that will destroy any hope of moving toward a collaborative community.

Stronger Together

If you're in a leadership position, you know your staff looks to you for guidance and strength. A big part of your responsibility is to lead by your actions. Here are two leadership perspectives I really like:

> Managers light a fire under people. Leaders light a fire in people.
>
> –Kathy Austin

> Managers do things right. Leaders do the right things.
>
> –Warren Bennis

As an educational leader, part of your job is to inspire the people around you to push themselves—and, in turn, those staff members will turn the school into a great place to work. To do this, you must provide opportunities for others to shine and take the lead. Empowerment is a mighty tool; how will you use it?

If you're a classroom teacher, your students want to be inspired. Kids don't come to school to watch their teachers work. Shifting the heavy lifting from teacher to student will shift the instruction from passive to active. Active learning involves collaboration and creativity. Collaborative opportunities will increase your students' higher-order reasoning and understanding. John Holt said, "Learning is not the product of teaching. Learning is the product of the activity of learners." Our job as educators is to make the classroom as dynamic as the world around us. The world around us is working collaboratively to solve problems--some of which we don't even know yet--and we need to prepare our students for that world.

Collaboration is a Win-Win Situation. It ensures all voices are heard and that a mutually agreeable outcome occurs. Individuals in leadership are striving for win-win situations all the time. This doesn't mean everyone gets exactly what they want. The goal is to find an acceptable solution for all parties. When you identify and implement a win-win solution, everyone leaves the situation with a sense of accomplishment.

Any time decisions need to be made, or individual needs are different, there's likely to be disagreement. You've heard the old saying, "You are either part of the problem or part of the solution." When you strive to make a situation win-win, you're part of the solution. Being a part of the solution means building trust and earning respect from colleagues and stakeholders. Also, when your staff and students see you consistently working to find a win-win solution, they'll be more understanding when you are forced to make swift decisions without asking for input first.

In a collaborative community, teachers, students, administrators, and families are all on the same team working toward the same goals. It may not always feel like you're on the same team, but ultimately, we all want students to learn, grow, and succeed.

When working toward a win-win solution, start by understanding the other person(s) concerns or perspective. Explore or discuss what all members of the discussion want and believe. With this information, you can explain your reasoning or position and start to build a solution that will benefit all. A successful win-win solution must happen so that all viewpoints and solutions are heard and shared efficiently. Saying you're on the same team is one thing; acting like it is another.

Once you have understood the other person(s) concerns or perspectives, separate it from the participant. Suppose the person feels like you are questioning them individually rather than challenging their concern or perspective. In that case, they are likely to feel backed into a corner and might not communicate fully. If you need more information, ask probing questions to allow the other person(s) the opportunity to explain. Also, don't be afraid to ask them directly what they want to achieve. The more information you have, the easier and clearer it becomes to resolve the situation with a win-win decision. Once both parties have had the chance to share, you must refocus the conversations on the key points or agenda items. This shows all involved that you understand the other person(s) position while also taking the next step toward a solution.

Once you have agreed on the key points, make it clear the next steps are finding an agreement that works for all. If a win-win solution cannot be reached, agree to resume the discussion later; allowing more time to generate ideas and reflect on implementation.

Other tips for developing a collaborative community that strives toward reaching win-win resolutions are:

- Revisit goals often: Continually focusing on the key points of meetings/discussions is critical to keeping the dialog on point. During the discussion, you can review steps already taken and tweak suggestions to create solutions that support and foster win-win scenarios. The more you stay focused on the goals, the more you will create opportunities for solutions.
- Visit possible solutions: As you review goals, discuss possible compromises. Make sure that everyone is open to any and all possibilities because they might lead to solutions. Solutions might be closer than you expect. You won't know this until or unless you visit all possible solutions early in the process.
- Don't take things personally: YES–this is easier said than done. But by not taking things personally, we separate our ego and the pain of decisions gone awry from the issue at hand; we stay focused on the key points in front of us.
- No assumptions: Assumptions have no place in a win-win resolution. When you assume (you have heard it before), you make an A** out of U and ME. Assumptions waste time and energy, create confusion, diminish trust, lead to disappointment, and undermine decision-making. All efforts put forth should focus on enhancing the next steps in the decision-making process and be direct, open, honest, and transparent.
- Believe there is a solution: If you enter a decision-making meeting or conversation without the belief you can reach a solution, there is no reason to have the meeting/discussion. You will quickly become

frustrated and experience a self-fulfilling prophecy.

- Put aside "winning": You can't have a mindset of wanting it all when working toward a win-win solution. The win-win solution is supposed to mutually benefit all parties to increase positive results. Even if the other party "gets" more, you have to view the resolution as a compromise.

Working in a community that strives toward win-win solutions is an environment built on trust and focused on the common good. Our goal is to educate our students, and no one can do that alone. By collaborating, we can provide a well-rounded education for all.

The heart of collaboration is about how to Engage everyone; every teacher, every leader, every student. It will take a variety of instructional strategies and resources to meet individual needs. When there is collaboration and everyone is involved, we must ensure individuals solve, think critically, and promote reflective learning. Involving all voices and individuals is the key to collaboration. Collaboration is not a few people doing all the work for the group. It is about promoting social development and the group responsibility of all participants.

Some key elements when reflecting on whether or not all voices are heard include asking the group these questions:

- Are we caring about individuals' social and emotional needs?

- Do we model positive attitudes and enhance enthusiasm?
- Do we treat all individuals fairly in our decision-making?

We are trying to ensure everyone is included in a collaborative culture. This inclusive feeling is not by chance; it takes work and time to develop. A culture of "everyone" is built on the foundation that our goal in schools is to promote fairness and respect.

As a staff, pride yourself on:

- Modeling and promoting fairness, equity, and respect in all aspects of the school.
- Encouraging, supporting, and recognizing achievements.
- Highlighting student or staff contributions to culture.

Just as important as highlighting achievement, we must fairly respond to behaviors that are not aligning with the culture. The school is a community that belongs to everyone. Classrooms are filled with children's work; staff rooms are filled with support resources; the halls are filled with smiles and welcoming expressions. Collaboration is the core of a culture that doesn't just talk about community; it models it every day.

While it can be scary to try new things and be a Risk-Taker, once someone else jumps into an initiative or idea, it's a lot easier to follow.

Truly innovative educators and leaders support a culture of trust in risk-taking. They foster a culture that is warm, collaborative, and accessible to all. They encourage colleagues from any level of the organization to offer ideas. They create safe physical and emotional spaces for teachers to explore and develop innovative learning opportunities. This cultural shift encourages more collaboration and less competition among faculty. We engage staff and students in risk-taking because they are allowed to make mistakes. Let's face it, we all make mistakes, but are we creating an environment supportive of others doing so too?

Schools are filled with rules and policies. We need these for times when things go astray and teachers and students don’t meet our most basic expectations. Unfortunately, rules and policies support reactive leadership rather than transformative leadership.

Reactive leadership is focusing on the negative outcomes or consequences that occur if students or staff try something new. But we also need to make sure we focus on what happens when students and staff are taking risks appropriately and creatively. We need to encourage risk-taking while also ensuring students and staff continue to meet our basic expectations. Trying new collaborative skills or ideas can be intimidating, especially when so many of these efforts occur in a classroom or in front of peers. And with any new things, mistakes are inevitable; things are not always going to go as we hope. Leaders need to acknowledge these risks and communicate with all stakeholders that they appreciate and support any and all collaborative efforts, even the ones that do go as planned. Successful leaders will be there to help risk-takers celebrate their accomplishments and reflect on their mistakes.

Amy Edmondson is the Novartis Professor of Leadership and Management at the Harvard Business School. Her work supports the study of human interactions that lead to the creation of successful enterprises that contribute to the betterment of society. She says, "I have seen this first hand as a principal and district leader. Psychological safety means an environment in which it is safe to speak one's mind, discuss with openness and honesty what is and isn't working, make collective decisions, take risks, and fail—all things researchers tell us are required for deep organizational change and transformation." In my years as a principal I know this kind of safety doesn't come easily in schools. We have to build a trusting environment to take risks because many ideas may take time to develop. Trust is earned by action. Leaders lead by example and foster collaboration.

So how do district leaders support a risk-taking environment?

- Don't risk everything–taking a risk is for growth
- Know what you want and ask/plan for it
- Execute
- Practice and learn from errors

- Don't stop and don't worry about what others think

Here are some basic rules for taking smart risks:

- **Define smart risks and set limits:** We need to define what we mean by "smart risks." The last thing we want as leaders is for every staff member to just take a risk for the "heck of it" and jeopardize student learning or educator confidence and growth. That is not smart risk-taking.
- **Model risk-taking behavior:** School and district leaders can't just show staff what they do well. They must be willing to try something new and let staff observe their efforts. Try using new technology in staff meetings, social media, or professional development. Leaders cannot be afraid to show vulnerability to their staff. Doing so can result in big gains in school trust.
- **Create a safe environment for risk-taking:** Creating a safe environment means not punishing people who take smart, acceptable risks. As a principal for 11 years, I know the evaluation process well. Unfortunately, concern over teacher evaluations may deter from taking risks. School leaders must talk about taking smart risks in educator goal-setting meetings early in the year. They can encourage educators to try new instructional styles or incorporate new innovative tools into lessons. In their first meeting with the school leaders, if educators hear that one of their goals is to try new edtech tools, curriculum initiatives, and instructional styles, they will be more willing to do so and will likely feel supported to take other smart risks too. Leaders can further

support risk-taking by assuring teachers they will not be punished if the smart risks they take aren't successful. Using educators' goals and the evaluation process as a collaborative, coaching tool will create an encouraging community devoid of teacher concern and ripe with excitement to try new things.

- **Reward smart missteps:** To show that the school is serious about risk-taking, set up a structure that reviews missteps and celebrates the best attempts. Instead of just designing plans in the spring and summer that will focus on academic success, create plans that encourage risk-taking and celebrate attempts. Build time into every staff meeting for teachers to share something they've tried in the past month. They can share successes and/or missteps. Sharing missteps helps gather other ideas to increase collaboration and support further risk-taking.

When staff understand what smart risk-taking is, they will understand their comfort zones and deal with anxiety and uncertainty more easily. Creating a culture of risk-taking starts with preparation, vision, and taking a risk to do it.

Pause Moment:

Reflect on the following question: Now that you have the POWER to design and launch collaboration and develop a community of "Stronger Together" thinkers, what can you do to start planting the seeds of collaboration?

Chapter 10: Be Stronger Together

Individual commitment to a group effort—that is what makes a team work, a company work, a society work, a civilization work.

—Vince Lombardi, American Football Coach

School leaders are empowered to guide and direct staff; however, work gets accomplished at the peer level. Colleagues understand how an individual's actions impact the classroom and the other team members. Additionally, peers are more likely to confide in peers when they encounter obstacles in the way of their growth. A team dynamic creates a powerful and trusting relationship where feedback is more likely to be valued and appreciated.

When your school culture supports peer support, colleagues can influence each other to change a behavior or improve real-time instructional practices. Instantaneous support can encourage rapid development and growth to keep the school on the path to success.

Peer-to-peer support is one way to develop a collaborative mindset in a school. Many words get thrown around when talking about peers working together: "peer coaching," "peer mentoring," "instructional buddies," etc. Ultimately, peers working together is all about support. There is no power imbalance. It's an "Us" mentality; staff is there for each other. Peer support aims to help each person become a more effective educator for students. Support allows each participant to equally focus on their colleague's learning and development. The support may occur once or be ongoing. Peer support allows colleagues to bounce ideas off each other and overcome isolation.

Peer support is a practical learning approach because individuals use their resources and experiences to find solutions to questions together. Peers can explore possibilities they might not have considered previously. Peer collaboration and support is non-judgmental and based on trust. If feedback is part of the collaboration, it should be constructive, and focus on growth. Peer feedback offers a confidential network of colleagues supporting each other with real-time concerns and questions.

A few critical norms when creating a culture that encourages and celebrates peer support are:

- Form a relationship: Supporting each other (or many people), can't happen without building a relationship first.
- Focus on the positive: The point of supporting each other is for growth. Nothing will be accomplished with criticism. Don't let your collaboration turn into a gripe session. I understand sometimes you need to vent to let off a bit of steam. But if you want to invest in each other's growth, limit the complaining. Collaboration time should be productive and

helpful to support and implement suggestions into your own practice.

- Be a good listener: Collaborating is not forcing your own ideas and agendas onto others. Collaborating is listening to a concern or struggle and talking through it.
- Be open-minded: Educators who believe they do not need to grow usually consider peer support a waste of time. However, developing a culture of collaboration calls for individuals to be open to change, eager to give and receive feedback, and willing to appreciate new perspectives and alternative ways of acting and thinking.
- Be curious: Curiosity is the foundation of all learning. People with a genuine curiosity are willing to engage in conversations that push their thinking and teach them something they hadn't previously considered.
- Acknowledge efforts and build trust: Peer collaboration is not easy for everyone and shows trust and vulnerability. A little affirmation in the efforts goes a long way.
- Know yourself: Be as aware as possible of your own biases when supporting or giving feedback.
- Be real: We all want to help. However, don't promise more than you can deliver; this will decrease your credibility and only serve to hurt your colleague(s).

- Prioritize confidentiality: The goal of peer support is to improve practice in a non-evaluative setting. If a colleague finds out you're talking about their performance in another setting, the relationship and initiative will be questioned.

Peer Visits

Nine times out of ten, a classroom observation is evaluative and linked to classroom performance. What if we shifted this mindset and viewed classroom observations as less punitive?

In a collaborative culture, teachers visiting other classrooms is a form of professional development that improves teaching practices and student performance. This kind of collaboration can yield its greatest benefits when used to share instructional techniques and ideas between and among teachers.

Before any initiative involving peer visits is launched, psychological safety and a risk-taking culture must be developed. To effectively launch peer visits, the environment must nurture a collegial exchange of ideas and promote a certain level of trust. Teaching has, historically, been very isolating. Opening your classroom is very public and can be uncomfortable. Trust is essential, both in the colleague and the process. The goal of peer visits is not to make a colleague look bad, but to support mutual growth and lifelong learning.

Peer visits should be part of a pool of professional development opportunities. They can be very effective when teachers acquire new skills at conferences and want to model those new approaches for colleagues. The experience must be mutual. By observing the new skill, the visiting teacher is considering something new. Simultaneously, the practicing teacher has an additional set of eyes in the room to see things they did not, or could not. When the visiting teaching is giving feedback, it must be student-focused. The feedback should focus on how the instruction can improve.

Have the visiting teacher select one focus area for the peer observation. This will focus the post-observation feedback and make for a less overwhelming discussion. Some examples of peer visit focus areas are:

- Lesson preparation and organization
- Instructional strategies
- Classroom management
- Clarity
- Wait time
- Presentation skills
- Rapport with students
- Questioning techniques
- Checks for understanding

Peer visits are a powerful initiative for teachers to improve their practice. However, simply having teachers visit other classrooms will not serve to improve instruction and, ultimately, learner experiences. This initiative must be structured for emotional safety and productivity. It is good practice to have peers sit down before the visit to establish what they will be observing and what, if anything, the practicing teacher would like their colleague to consider.

Some questions to guide the pre-meeting are:

- What is the purpose of the visit?
- What is the intended learning outcome?
- How will the learning activities support the intended learning outcome?
- What, if anything, would you like me to focus on in this observation?
- How would you like feedback, if at all?

For peer visits to work, there needs to be time: time to meet and establish the visit's goals, time to plan the visit, time for the visit, and time to debrief after the visit. Expecting teachers to use their already limited planning time will result in a less than fruitful experience and will likely be met with resistance. This initiative requires leadership support. Providing this opportunity will increase trust and collegiality among staff. Show the staff you are invested in the process by asking questions about the peer visits when you see them. Ask:

- How's it going?
- What's working?
- What can I do to help?

Collaborative Journeys

Peer visits are one way to get colleagues working with one another, collaborative journeys in the school are another. Collaborative journeys are approaches for administrators and educators to work together to improve practice, support improvement in educator instruction, and be present in the classrooms. Being present as a leader is critical in building a collaborative school community. The two collaborative journeys I recommend are Learning Walks and Instructional Rounds.

Learning Walks. A Learning Walk is a brief, structured classroom visit that provides school administrators and teachers opportunities to reflect on what students are learning and how students are engaging in the curriculum. A Learning Walk is conducted by school-based educators working with the building administrator (Feeney, 2014). Once the Learning Walk team is developed, a structure is followed for consistency. The school administrator often selects a data-collection instrument for the team to collect and organize observed information. The Learning Walk instrument can be a checklist, narrative template, or electronic photo device. The goal of the Learning Walk process is to develop a deep understanding of teaching and learning and allow educators to reflect on professional practice (City, 2011). Additionally, educators can reflect and identify how to incorporate those practices into their instruction.

A Learning Walk has three components, beginning with a pre-walk meeting (Lemons & Helsing, 2009). The goal of the pre-walk meeting is for the learning team to identify the instructional focus to be observed during the walk and which classrooms to visit (Feeney, 2014). Depending on the team, a short discussion on why classrooms have been selected may be necessary. Some examples of an observation learning focus can include, but are not limited to: questioning strategies, classroom management, differentiated instruction, cooperative learning, wait time, and classroom development.

The classroom visit follows the pre-walk meeting and should last between 5–10 minutes. Next, the team should split up into small groups to visit multiple classrooms (Jove, 2011). Team members will take notes of the identified focus while in the classroom. The process for classroom visits should remain consistent throughout the observations. Student questions can also be developed in the pre-meeting and then asked during the Learning Walk.

Following the observations, the Learning Walk team assembles for a post-meeting (Feeney, 2014). During the post-meeting, each observing team member shares his/her observations and provides evidence to support any claim made about the observation. In addition, the team members identify instructional tendencies, patterns, areas of instructional strength, and areas for educator growth. After sharing, the team members reflect and can offer recommendations to the administrator about next steps for the school. Marzano and Watters (2005) believe that the more information a school leader has, the more capable they are to lead and support teachers.

The Learning Walk process allows for educator collaboration around best practices and administrator opportunity to observe classroom practices and other areas in which educators work. Learning Walks are not recommended for an educator's formal observation. Rather, data from the visit can help shape an understanding about the teacher's practices and support the evaluation process.

Instructional Rounds. Instructional Rounds are an orderly observation method for educators to collaborate and improve instruction. The Instructional Rounds as a method of observation, are similar to Learning Walks; however, the focus of Instructional Rounds is firmly on the instructional core and the "relationship between the teacher, the student, and the content" (City 2009, p. 21). Successful rounds generally focus on "one rich problem based on students' learning instead of the classroom teaching" (p. 22-23).

The Instructional Rounds process is adapted from the medical rounds model that doctors use in hospitals (City, 2011). The medical profession incorporates rounds with physicians to teach and share knowledge based on diagnosis and treatment of patients. Instructional Rounds help educators look closely at what is happening in classrooms for specific students in a systematic, purposeful, and focused way. Educators who participate in rounds should expect to learn, whereas, in formal or informal observations, only the person being observed is anticipated to learn (City, 2011; Roegman & Reihl, 2012).

As with Learning Walks, the building administrator is part of the team. The educators' focus during this process is on growth in instructional practice. The administrator's focus should be on learning more about their teachers to assist in supporting their growth through the evaluation process. Teachers can use skills observed during rounds to improve practice.

The initial step in the Instructional Rounds process is to meet as a team and identify a problem of practice. Then, as a group, they look for the problem in practice during the rounds (Marzano; 2011; Roberts 2012). The problem of practice focus is to "gather information directly on the work of teaching and learning" (City, 2009, p. 99). It is important to note that during the rounds, educators are asked to make observations and describe what is being seen during instruction--rather than making judgments.

Following the rounds, participating educators meet and debrief what they observed. The purpose of the debrief is to discuss the collected evidence of the group and what learning occurred. During this step, educators should describe, not judge, the data that is relevant to the problem of practice and listen and learn from colleagues to analyze any emerging patterns. Finally, educators will identify the next level of work for the school and their own practice (Marzano, 2011; Roberts, 2012).

Learning Walks and Instructional Rounds are both collaborative in nature and are intended to produce educator growth. Compared to formal and informal observations, these methods are not direct observations of an educator by an administrator. Learning Walks and Instructional Rounds are observations that serve to provide a view of the school that a building administrator would not otherwise get from a single observation alone. While Learning Walks and Instructional Rounds will assist administrators in accumulating a running account of teacher instruction, student-teacher interactions, and student outcomes in the building, the main function of these practices is to get the pulse of the school.

You may be wondering how these collaborative journeys will enhance the culture of collaboration at a school? Consider that Learning Walks and Instructional Rounds will:

- Provide opportunities for district leaders, school administrators, instructional coaches, and teachers to have enhanced dialogue about teaching and learning.
- Assist the school in developing a common language around instruction and instructional methods.
- Allow administrators to build a professional development calendar around the greatest needs of the teachers in the building.
- Ensure the effectiveness of ideas towards building a culture of collaborative feedback.

- Affirm accomplishments and add clarity to the challenges of a school.

Peer visits and collaborative journeys enable staff to learn, describe, and identify effective teaching. Learning throughout the building is an opportunity to dive into problems and discuss solutions. This level of collaboration will create a common understanding and language between all staff members and enhance the community of learners. Peer visits and collaborative journeys are not opportunities to evaluate teachers. Rather, they are opportunities to engage in collaborative discussions focused on the work being done in the school.

Pause Moment:

Reflect on the following questions: Do I utilize my colleagues as a resource to support my growth as an educator? What can I do to increase collaboration with colleagues?

Chapter 11
Empowering Students

Learning is not the product of teaching. Learning is the product of the activity of learners.

—John Holt, American Author and Educator

One of the keys to academic achievement is active collaboration and student voice. According to research, personalized, collaborative, connected learning experiences enhance student engagement. Student engagement drives student success. What makes active student collaboration authentic and relevant is the integration of student voice in the classroom. With an increase in active learning, educators can take classroom experiences to the next level and enhance student performance. In this chapter, we'll dive into strategies that will increase student verbal participation and empower educators with the tools necessary to create a culture of content creators and excited learners.

Engagement and active learning are hot topics in education today. However, if you look at a classroom in the 1950's, you'd see desks in rows, a teacher in the front of the room doing the talking, books out on the desks, and students consuming the lesson. Should classrooms in the 21st century look the same? The answer to that question should be a resounding NO. But think about it, do our classrooms look the same? Unfortunately, many of them do. In today's classrooms, too often, we teach by disseminating information that we expect students to consume. However, in no other part of a student's life are they expected to sit and absorb information by themselves and then try to replicate a task. So why are we asking them to do this in the classroom?

Edgar Dale was an educator and researcher. He created the Learning Pyramid which allows teachers to understand how to increase the retention rate of learners by involving the learners. He found that students tend to remember 90 percent of what they say or do in a lesson, but only 10 percent of what they read, 20 percent of what they hear, and 30 percent of what they see. Benjamin Franklin said, "Tell me, I forget. Teach me, I remember. Involve me, I learn." Are we involving students in their learning?

Active collaborative learning refers to the idea that students are actively engaged in the learning process rather than passively absorbing content. Students engage in the material they study through reading, writing, talking, listening, and reflecting. For example, students can solve problems, answer questions, formulate questions of their own, discuss, explain, debate, or brainstorm during class. The benefits of such activities include improvement in critical-thinking skills, increase in retention and transfer of new information, increase in motivation, and improvement in interpersonal skills.

Examine forward-thinking companies like *Google, Apple*, and *Facebook*. These companies pride themselves on a culture of flexibility, collaboration, team-based brainstorming, project-based tasks, and creativity. Active learning can provide classrooms and students with these very same things while also serving to increase student participation, engagement, and retention. Furthermore, giving students ownership of their own learning gives them the knowledge to talk about and share their learning through their own voices.

To enhance a risk-taking mindset in the classroom, we must move to a "We Did" mindset. Teachers are often asked to write objectives or "I can" statements on the board before the learning begins. However, education is evolving right before our eyes. We should be focusing on what the students did together; collaboratively. Sharing "We did" statements after a lesson about what was created or learned during class is a way to establish a collaborative environment in the classroom. Designing activities geared towards paired activities, small informal groups, and cooperative student projects will begin to shift the lessons towards being more active.

To make this shift at the classroom level, teachers should have specific strategies that make curriculum and collaborative lessons an ongoing component of their learning environment. Making regular and meaningful connections to content and creative activities will assist both the educator and learner in this shift. For teachers to increase collaboration, students should have regular opportunities to talk with classmates about the work that they are doing, as well as time to share strategies that worked best. Lessons and projects should be designed to make connections between the classroom and the real world.

Moving to a more collaborative, learner-centered classroom will infuse creative thinking into the lessons and increase student excitement for learning. When students become self-directed and take charge of their learning, they work together in an assortment of ways. This gives them the time to self-manage, self-assess, retain, and apply information.

Shifting the heavy lifting in learning from teacher to student will shift instruction to be more active and creative. It will also serve to increase higher-order reasoning and understanding. Our job as educators is to make the classroom as dynamic as the world around us. We must shift the classroom mindset from statements like "Students will be able to..." to the mentality and expectation of "We Did" statements. This shift will provide a Stronger Together culture not just in the school, but in the classroom too.

Moving the classroom from a place where students are consuming information to a place where collaborative learning is actively occurring, will not happen overnight. But the following strategies will help teachers and students make this shift successfully:

- Have students work in teams to search *Google Scholar* for an article that supports current research or addresses an assigned content topic. Once they've read their articles, students can work with a classmate(s) to create and share a brief video or multimedia presentation in which they summarize their thoughts and key points.
- Ask teams of students to find a website related to a topic being covered in class. Have them think critically about the information they find on the website and evaluate it. Students can discuss findings on a discussion board, *Google Drive*, or break into groups. The goal is to open students' eyes to the variety and relative reliability of the

information they find on the open web.

- Start implementing makerspaces in the classroom. Makerspaces are another way to provide creative time and space for students to build prototypes, explore questions, fail, retry, bounce ideas off one another, and work together.
- Have students document their thinking in the design process for any project. They can take photos and video articulating their thoughts and how they came to the decisions they made. This thinking process and video creation can be part of a student presentation.
- Have students create a project preview in *Flipgrid* (*Flipgrid.com*). Present it to students as making a trailer to their project just like you would see for a movie. This grid can be made public, and if posted a week before the project showcase, it can build excitement and intrigue for the projects as the students hype their work.
- When a new year begins, students have new or restored hopes and dreams; for the year, for themselves, for what the future brings. *Padlet* (*padlet.com*) is a tool where a teacher can create a digital pinboard that can be shared with students and families. Teachers can create a template and then email the unique *Padlet* link to families. Ask students

what they "hope" for the year. The answers can give you a baseline for your planning and show students you value them as a part of the class. For example, you could start the year by displaying the "Board of Hopes" and have students share theirs to create a culture of togetherness. It may also inspire classmates to help each other reach their dreams.

- Ask students what *they* want in the classroom. Again, you can use *Padlet* or *Flipgrid* for this activity. You can even ask them about the structure of classroom centers or suggestions for books they want to read. Students are walking into YOUR room, but it's THEIR learning. Asking them for input in designing the space will give them a sense of control and ownership in their own learning.
- Anyone with a phone has either used, overused, or seen silly GIFs that make people laugh. GIFs are so popular that many students might even have a GIF keyboard on their phone. You can also use one of the many free GIF sites on the web. Pose a question to your students and ask them to send a GIF as their answer. Email the question to your students and students' families depending on their age. This could be a great way to learn about your students' feelings on returning to school after an extended break. Day one could be going through the GIF collection. This is a fun way to get an inside look,

without prying, into how your students are feeling.

- One of my favorite ways for student collaboration and building a Stronger Together mindset is the educational game platform Breakout EDU. This platform challenges students to work together to solve academic problems. Breakout EDU engaging activities rely on students working collaboratively and exercising their SEL and 4C skills while the teacher can genuinely observe the student-owned learning. The activity itself is similar to an escape room designed for the classroom. Students will often come up against a wrong answer and have to use perseverance and work together in order to fail forward and eventually succeed. The risks they take along the way to getting the correct answer helps to highlight that failure is not permanent and being wrong is part of the learning process. To learn more about it check out the website.

As teachers begin to learn more, classroom projects should become more dynamic in design thinking and production. The next step is allowing dynamic projects to become part of the learning culture. This shift will require a coordinated effort between mindset, behaviors, and skills.

Creativity must be infused into student learning. I often see teachers preparing projects for students before they assign them, e.g., cutting out all the pieces to make a snowman, or setting up all the equipment for a science lab. By doing this beforehand, teachers are removing creativity options. Yes, it may help the classroom run more smoothly if every child's material is already cut out or set-up ahead of time, but then everything looks the same. Not having everything prepped in advance is a good thing. Giving students all the supplies needed to create a snowman or lab and letting them do it on their own is active learning. It allows students to become critical, creative thinkers.

Think back to *Google* and *Facebook*. Collaboration and a Stronger Together mindset is how they went from an idea to changing our world. Moving toward a collaborative, learner-centered classroom will change your student's world.

Learning is not a spectator sport. Students do not learn by sitting in a classroom listening to teachers, memorizing prepackaged assignments, and regurgitating answers. Students learn by talking about what they're doing, relating to new experiences, and applying them to their daily lives. Empower students to collaborate by welcoming their lens and creativity into the classroom; their success will thank you for it.

Pause Moment:

Reflect on the following questions.

- Do I allow risk taking in my classroom/ school?
- Do I take risks as an educator?
- What can I do to increase risk taking in my classroom/school?

Chapter 12
It Takes a Village

It takes a village to educate a child.

–Nigerian Proverb

Collaboration involves all stakeholders inside and outside of the schoolhouse walls. Schools cannot move forward with a collaborative culture if the voices of all members are not heard. I couldn't write a book about collaboration and being Stronger Together without modeling this. What follows will not be my voice. Rather, it will be the voices of the other members of a school community: teachers, committee members and parents. These stories and messages will focus on Stronger Together as a mindset for all and the positive effects it has on students from every angle.

Caring Class & Community

Written by Christine Bemis, Teacher
Follow her at @ChristineBemis2

My name is Christine Bemis, and I am the proud educator of primary school children. From humble beginnings as the second youngest child in a large Irish American family, I aim to bring joy into the lives of the students and families with whom I work. I do this to ensure they have the best education possible under my tutelage. I call this work, heartwork.

For as long as I can remember, I've always wanted to work with children, and going into education was the most logical path. My work with children started in my early teens. I volunteered as a big sister for the local *Big Brother/Big Sister* organization. From there, I was a literacy volunteer at a local summer program and a mentor/tutor to children living in foster and residential congruent care settings. My approach always focused on creating a caring, loving environment that supported youth through connection, compassion, acceptance of others, and community.

Strong connections with families are an integral part of being an educator. It takes intentional and deliberate work to understand family traditions, cultures and what makes a student's family just that; a family. Diversity is a beautiful thing and having the privilege to work with students from all walks of life is, in my humble opinion, an honor to be nurtured and embraced.

The first step in getting to know my students' families is what I commonly refer to as "walk-abouts." Every year, I start visiting all of my students' homes, apartments, and shared living quarters during the last two weeks of summer vacation. This activity demonstrates the importance of meeting families where they are prior to the start of the school year. I strive to get to know students and their families in a positive, joyful, lighthearted way.

I usually conduct "walk-abouts" on the weekends and include a welcome bag for each student with age-appropriate trinkets. I also present each of them with a personal handwritten welcome message. Ziploc bags, a few items from the local dollar store, and an inexpensive notecard are not a far stretch to start a strong home-school relationship.

It's always gratifying to see the kindness and thanks we are met with from caregivers on these "walk-abouts." These visits allow me to get a glimpse into students' lives, where they live, and sometimes a taste of the food they eat each night. Families and students are proud to share their culture with us and are *always* happy to welcome us into their homes. Stories about families' backgrounds, traditions, and beliefs are often part of our discussions. These are meaningful listening opportunities for me as I get to connect with my students. Family members have expressed that I am there for their student's best interest and have given them a voice in their child's educational future. Trust is gained in these visits and thus sets the foundation for collaboration and a shared investment in the academic success of their child. "Walk-abouts" also serve to reduce some of the fears and jitters associated with the inevitable return to school.

Many years ago, I saw my husband, a carpenter by trade, filling up a large bucket with tools for an upcoming woodworking job. An idea was born...give students their own bucket to fill up with the tools they're going to need to be successful in the classroom. I would tie the student buckets into our caring, class, community-building activities.

Each student receives a white, 5-gallon bucket; similar to the ones you'd find at any home improvement store. My husband and I, well mostly my husband, make a top for the bucket. One side of the top is made of cushy foam and decorative material, while the other side is given a whiteboard-type finish. The cushy side serves as a seat and the reverse side is a lap pad for writing and/or creating. Students fill the buckets with any of the tools they'll need in class: books, markers, pens, pencils, etc. All students use the seats at their respective desks; "bucket seats" as I call them.

We start off the year learning positive affirmations like *I am smart...I can do hard things...I choose to be happy...I am limitless...* These phrases become ingrained in our daily conversations and students are encouraged to write these affirmations on the outside of their "bucket seats." They serve as great reminders of a growth mindset and support the vision of our classroom as a place that has a strong sense of connection, positivity, and community.

As time goes on, newly learned phrases, class chants, and slogans are added to their respective buckets. Colorful, creative, and unique are just a few adjectives to describe these seats. Additionally, they are an impactful tool supporting the Stronger Together mindset.

As the year progresses, my students participate in regularly scheduled meetings with younger students to teach them newly learned skills. They travel with their full "bucket seats" to younger-aged classrooms and conduct mini learning sessions focused on sharing a newly acquired skill. The seats travel easily and are carried proudly with confidence and ease. Sharing skills via the "bucket seats" fosters a strong sense of classroom and school-wide community.

By the end of the year, the "bucket seats" become a visual representation of the diversity of the classroom as well as the cohesiveness of a wide range of learners who have developed lifelong skills in communication, sharing, and literacy. None of this happens without practice and a shared investment in the learning process for the betterment of others. The students take their "bucket seats" home at the end of the year as a well-loved keepsake of our time together.

But to get students to the finish line and model learning for the younger students in the building, praise, support, and encouragement must be ever-present components of the daily classroom. In fact, they are so omnipresent that they become classroom chants. Positivity chants that use words and hand gestures are often practiced at the beginning of the day and are woven through all of our lessons, including class meetings, pair-share skits, and daily closure circles. For example, the first chant is three words:

- Praise
- Support
- Encouragement

We say these three words and then clap five times; two slow claps followed by three quick claps.

Praise, Support, Encouragement claaap, claaap, clap, clap, clap.
Praise, Support, Encouragement claaap, claaap, clap, clap, clap.
Praise, Support, Encouragement claaap, claaap, clap, clap, clap.

To show excitement for risk-taking and/or a job well done, students use their hands and face to mimic the word "Wow." Students make a W with their fingers on both hands and put them to either side of their face. Each hand represents a "W" and the child's face is the "O." This represents a WOW moment celebrating another student's accomplishments. This is a wonderful way to provide affirmation quietly while building confidence and enjoyment in learning both individually and collectively.

The last chant is also done with hand gestures and focuses on three words: caring, class, and community. The left hand makes a "C" and the right hand makes a backward "C". We hold up the two "Cs" representing caring and class before bringing both hands together to make a heart. When we do, we say, "Community."

We repeat 3 times:

Caring, Class, and Community.
Caring, Class, and Community.
Caring, Class, and Community.

Stronger Together means just that, together...with educators, support staff, students, families, and caregivers all working together for the betterment of others. When we operate and unite as one strong force, our students benefit greatly; academically, socially, and emotionally. In return, our world becomes richer, wiser, and more connected than ever before.

All Voices Matter

Written by Merylina Santiago Asselin
School Counselor at Westfield High School

2018 Western MA Counselor Association School Counselor of the Year
2019 Mass School Counselor Association School Counselor of the Year

My name is Merylina Santiago Asselin, School Counselor at Westfield High School in Western Massachusetts. I was born and raised in San Juan, Puerto Rico. I am the middle sister of a trio of caring individuals, all of whom work in the field of social work/ counseling. My career began as an Assistant Director of Admissions at Springfield College in the 1990s, where I subsequently completed a Master's in Education after earning a bachelors in Business Administration/ Psychology from the same institution. As an admissions counselor, I had visited countless high schools in New England, Puerto Rico, and the US Virgin Islands in search of the right matches for Springfield College. The high school adolescents and their needs motivated me to pursue a career in school counseling. I became a certified/ licensed School Counselor in May 2000. I have been a school counselor ever since.

For the last two years, I have served as Co-President of the Western Massachusetts Counselor Association (WMCA). WMCA is an affiliate of the Massachusetts School Counselor Association. Currently, we have over 150 members throughout Western Massachusetts and

Northern Connecticut. The objective of WMCA is to bring together professionals in the school counseling and college admissions arena to collaborate and share new trends in the field.

I am currently one of seven school counselors at Westfield High School (WHS). Before Westfield High School, I was a school counselor in Chicopee, MA for eight years. WHS has an enrollment of 1100 students giving me a caseload of about 200 students in grades 10-12. As a school community, we support our students socially, athletically, and academically. Our teachers and counselors serve as coaches and advisors. Through our work as school counselors, we create bonds with our students that go beyond our office walls. We are cheerleaders on the sidelines, driver license study group facilitators, and a listening ear when life seems out of control.

School counselors are essential members of the school's leadership team. They, together with school administration, teachers and staff, create a school culture of success for *all* students. Our main role is to advocate, support, and assist students in managing emotions and setbacks. We aim to empower students to achieve academic success. Additionally, school counselors assist students in exploring post-secondary opportunities by creating a college and career-ready environment within the school. High school counselors are highly trained individuals in child and adolescent development who promote success for all students by encouraging self-reflection. As school counselors, we provide a safe place for students to be themselves and explore the countless opportunities beyond high school. This brings a feeling of belonging to schools and establishes a culture of collaboration.

Collaboration within the school is vital. School counselors, teachers, and administrators must form an alliance to improve and support student achievement and social-emotional development. The relationships we foster must be built on trust and respect.

As high school counselors, we work jointly with teachers to provide the space to deliver a developmentally appropriate curriculum that focuses on college readiness, career exploration, and social/emotional development for all students. School counselors provide counseling lessons in collaboration with departments during the year.

Lessons delivered included:

- Transition and Getting to know you- Grade 9
- My Success Habits & Support Networks- Grade 10
- College Fit and Supermatch- Grade 11
- My College Application & Being Career Ready- Grade 12

The collaboration amongst counselors, students, and families is the catalyst for student success. Often, the counselor is the primary contact for parents to connect with the school. The connection between school and home is vital in creating partnerships to support student success. It has been proven that healthy home/ school relationships contribute to better grades, better attendance and better behavior. When families feel supported at school, positive outcomes follow.

The disconnect between school and home, at times, can be due to language and cultural barriers. As a bilingual counselor, I often bridge the gap between Spanish-speaking families and schools. Having counselors or school personnel who can assist families in various languages is advantageous to any school district.

Partnerships between students, families, teachers, principals, school counselors, school staff, and coaches are vital for student success. Students need us to provide a school culture that is positive, vibrant, supportive, and strong. When we all work together to achieve a common goal, we are all Stronger Together.

We Are the Village

Written By Sylvia Hall, Parent, and Founder of GAB-on!
Follow her work with GAB-on! at: @GAB_on

Parent: "How was your day?"
Child: "Fine."
Parent: "What did you do in school today?"
Child: "Nothing."

Anyone who has kids, knows kids, or was a kid, recognizes this dialogue. I'm guessing it's the most popular (and fastest) conversation of our time; heard millions of times everyday worldwide. There's no authentic question, no real answer, and yet it checks-off a box every night; a family check-in. I actually believe that parents who ask these questions really do want to know about their child's day. I also think that kids really want to tell them. A student spending 7 hours a day at school must be doing a whole lot of something. So, not only is this check-in entirely predictable and unproductive, it comes with a huge opportunity cost.

I have two teenagers in public school and it's been a fascinating journey thus far. Our oldest was diagnosed at an early age with learning differences. When the neurologist shared his diagnoses with us, many started with "dis" or "dys," or something entirely foreign to us; it was very overwhelming. As is a fairly typical timeline, by 3rd grade his challenges became more apparent as the learning became more complex. As a result, we decided to move our son from the local public school to a private school for children with learning differences. The decision was a good one initially, but as time went on, circumstances arose that made us realize the decision wasn't as good as we thought. After two years at private school, we moved our son back to public school in a different state. He immediately began thriving and continues to do so five years later. As a parent, I often hold my breath when reading about the struggles of kids who learn differently, but I want you to know he has incredible support, he's in his community, and he's happy. Exhale.

I'm sharing a tiny piece of our experience with education because it started our family on a completely unexpected journey of special education, general education, family engagement, student agency, mental health, and entrepreneurship. The struggle that our son was experiencing in school was heartbreaking and given his significant working memory challenge, we were unable to communicate with him about what was actually going on during his school day. Of course, we recognized that he was in core classes with lessons, activities, and events throughout the day. We received regular emails from the school and teachers about areas of study and homework reminders. But what we didn't have was our son's perspective on his day, what he experienced, how he felt challenged, where he found joy, and all of the 'in between stuff' that shapes the student's school day. As parents, we wanted to hear our son's perspective, about his day, from him. So, we created something small for our son that has (almost accidentally) become a platform for so many. That is how GAB-on! was born (https://gab-on.com). GAB-on! is a platform that gets a family talking - about school -

every day. It was inspired by our son *but* built for ALL kids.

Getting our family talking - about school - every day is essential to our students' success and connection to the school community. It started with a Google sheet for our son and then, as we sat around our dinner table *actually talking about school*, our daughter requested to use it too. After a few months, our daughter's teacher asked to use it for her entire class. Then another teacher, and another, and then a school.

It's been amazing to see the impact that talking with our kids about school has had on our family connectedness, their social and emotional development, and their academics. To feel a connection with school enhances the Stronger Together mindset that allows for education to be a journey, not a one way street.

The most accurate predictor of a student's academic achievement is the extent to which their family is involved in his/her education.

–Anne Henderson, Annenberg Institute for School Reform.

We were simply parents wanting to connect with our kids yet, along our journey of collaborating with educators, researchers, doctors, parents, and students, what we discovered about the impact of family engagement on a child's academic, social, and emotional development was astounding. The collective relationship of educator - student - family is the magic ingredient for a child's agency, higher education, work-readiness, and life success. For me, that defines Stronger Together.

How educators *and* parents *and* students communicate in a triangular format, work together, and connect, not only creates opportunities for that student's future in education and career, it also lays the foundation for what relationships can look like. The impact of this collaboration gives them agency to collaborate with others in and outside of school. I want to share some life-altering outcomes for students that I have learned over the years when families are engaged in their child's education.

Relationships can fuel student growth, resilience, and education equality.

–Dr. Pam Cantor, Turnaround for Children.

I like to think about relationships as the fuel for all things moving forward. Family engagement can be talked about on many levels in education, from a parent phone call to inviting families to collaborate on education policies in the district. But I want to talk about family engagement in the context of a student's day-to-day experience in school.

There are many barriers to family engagement that can include time, language, fear, access, and experience. But there is no better expert on a student than their parent or guardian. From an educator's perspective, it is critical for the success of a student and the success of a classroom/school to partner with families and to do so consistently.

Educators engaging and collaborating with families results in student agency. Student agency builds critical thinking, relationships, and self-awareness. It is agency that allows students to recognize when they need to ask for help (academically, socially, and emotionally) and who they can ask. It builds the capacity to understand that overcoming obstacles and adversity is rarely done alone and that they have the skills and courage to build a community around them to help them achieve their goals.

> Promoting student voice can be of enormous benefit to the teacher's craft as well.
>
> –Eric Toshalis and Michael J. Nakkula (2012)

When a student talks with their parents consistently over time about their school experience, sharing their struggles and their joys, it begins to display patterns of what subjects or activities get them excited, where they naturally drift, and how they see their own potential. It creates a family connectedness that builds confidence in a child to develop agency. It results in a more engaged student in school and allows a parent to reimagine their child's possibilities for higher education, a passionate career, and a fulfilled life.

Imagine a student gets super excited about a lesson at school. The topic appeals to them, and they see an opportunity to learn and grow within it. To be Stronger

Together, we must work on ways as a family and school to get them to share these experiences beyond their time in school. As a child talks about their day, their understanding of the subject matter improves, their confidence grows, and a feeling of connectedness builds.

Sharing family connectedness from a parent's lens is part of the Stronger Together mantra. When students come to school feeling good about themselves, supported at home, and confident in their ability, their participation and energy exudes in the classroom; it might even be contagious.

Here are some additional voices talking about collaborative communities:

> How you treat each other matters. Your community matters. Relationships matter. As we look around at the world today, it is sometimes really challenging to believe that. Teaching our youth how to navigate the ups and downs of a community of different individuals is critical to their success and happiness in life. Culture is not all pep talks and recognitions. Culture has bumps, bruises, and ice packs. How we pull back together as a community and repair our "culture tapestry" tells an important story about who we are and who we want to be.
>
> -Kelly Mullen-Martin, MSEd, CAGS AEL
> Elementary School Principal

With collaboration, typically siloed content areas become more cohesive and meaningful to students. Teachers, administrators, and all staff know that they contribute to students' learning experiences; they are invested and proud of their positions. Model in actions and build a curriculum that reinforces values. Have students participate in projects (rather than traditional assessments) that build community in and out of school.

-Bonnie Nieves
High School Teacher, Author of *Be Awesome on Purpose*, Founder of *Educate on Purpose*

School culture is an established set of norms based on core values and beliefs within a school that drives the behavior of everyone in the school environment. It is essential to build a collaborative school for consistency in ensuring all stakeholders stay focused on the school's mission. Teachers and other people need to learn how to develop intrinsic satisfaction for doing their jobs well, which they should be doing, and not be dependent on others for praise, which affects worthiness and morale.

-Donna McCance
Teacher/Leader

A collaborative culture is one where the attitudes of the school community come together. Adults working together is what is best for kids. We learn best from our peers. Many teachers have told me that all they want is to be recognized and respected by their administration. It is imperative that administrators are visible and recognize what our teachers are doing both in and out of the classroom. This, in turn, builds trust and rapport with the staff.

-Marina Kosak
Assistant Principal for Student Services, Glenbard South High School

Working together will take you farther than working alone! A collaborative school is leaving no one behind and has common goals to focus on. Live out the values that govern the operation of the school.

-Rolland Chidiac
Re-engagement Teacher

Everyone wants to feel valued. In a collaborative environment, everyone can contribute their unique strengths to work toward a shared goal and that helps foster a more positive school culture. Small, daily actions of authentic, sincere recognition go a long way toward assisting teachers in feeling valued.

-Shelli Ann
Librarian/Media Specialist

To read even more thoughts on collaborative communities from educators around the globe, check out the Twitter chat QR code. Contributors answered questions pertaining to the benefits of collaboration and how to encourage it in their classrooms and school buildings.

Pause Moment:

Reflect on the following question: Am I part of the village that supports students or am I just a singular support?

Chapter 13
Have Fun

Never, ever underestimate the importance of having fun.

–Randy Pausch, Professor at Carnegie Mellon University

How many times have you said, "Standards and Assessments and Data OH MY......." With the increasing pressure in our field, educators often find themselves needing to close the door just to get work done. This can turn our work into more of a compliance task rather than passion work. However, we must continue to search for creative ways to put the fun back in the work we do and find ways to stay connected with our colleagues. Find a way to tap into the talents and interests of staff and allow your team to show up excited for work. We can step outside of our comfort zones and ensure staff is bringing their unique personalities into the district amidst all the state and national mandates.

A "fun" work environment does not mean staff should cease taking work seriously. It does mean loosening staff up and improving their mood. Smiling more is never a bad thing. Allowing enjoyment at work makes (and keeps) staff happy and excited to get their hands dirty. Birthday celebrations, recognition of milestones, or "just because" celebrations provide temporary relief to work-related stress and allow employees to enjoy themselves. These things also breed a feeling of togetherness and positive culture in the building. A little gesture or a fun sign on the door in the morning may brighten someone's mood in such a way that their productivity increases.

I fully understand that staff can get irritated with each other from time-to-time. That's to be expected when you spend a lot of time with anyone. However, leadership needs to address these issues before tensions flare. A fun, healthy environment will allow staff to "police themselves." Employees will be able to work out their issues in an appropriate manner.

Too many schools don't entertain the idea of having fun in the building. School is serious. Data, evaluation, and lesson planning are often at the forefront of everything we do. Nonetheless, even the most formal school environment can reap the rewards of allowing staff to take pleasure and joy in their work day.

Many successful businesses have started working more enjoyable environments into their business plans; why can't schools? Here are some examples of highly successful businesses making the time and effort to have fun in the workplace:

Volkswagen turned a staircase into a giant, fully functioning piano keyboard, resulting in a 66 percent increase in employees choosing to take the stairs over the escalator. This one small, fun change transformed the way people behaved in a situation that would otherwise be a chore.

Hubspot's CEO has a small rooftop terrace where the team gathers for "refreshments" after work. The CEO believes that these meetings led to the company's success because they create a team bond and make work a more sociable place.

LinkedIn introduced the Walk & Talk to their meeting menus. Walk & Talks allow team members to take a stroll to catch up or have meetings. It's a great way to introduce some exercise into the work day, and it releases stress, improves health, and makes people happier. And it is nice to just take a break sometimes.

Yes, schools may not have the luxury of adding a staircase piano to the building or having refreshments on the roof, but that doesn't mean we can't brainstorm other ideas and add some fun into our workdays. A few school-appropriate ideas you CAN put into place tomorrow are:

Game Day Staff Meeting: Staff meetings are a way to get information out to everyone, but you can also do this in an email or shared document. Instead of disseminating information, use that hour to host a staff game day with activities ranging from trivia to video bowling or even corn hole in the hallway. Mix in funny, unique prizes to be displayed for continued bragging rights. Allowing staff to participate in some friendly workplace games can help build a greater sense of community.

Office Supply Team Challenge: Ahead of a staff meeting one year, I was at a loss for what to do. I didn't want to just talk about random school stuff just because we had a scheduled meeting. I went into the supply closet and grabbed an assortment of office supplies, and thought, "What can we do with these?" I remembered a high school science project where we had to build a structure out of a stick of balsa wood. How could I duplicate that in a team challenge? I split the staff into teams, gave each team an egg, and set up the office supply challenge. The rules were simple: Use up to 10 items to build a soft structure to see how high you could get the egg to drop and not break. We had a lot of laughs and, without thinking about it, improved our communication and critical-thinking skills.

Take "USies" with your staff and students: We are often"solo" in our profession. One teacher, one room. Do we have to highlight that? You say the word selfie, and so many images come into your mind (and some you don't want). But mostly, it is ONE person taking a photo of themselves with a smartphone so they can share it on social media. So let's stop highlighting the "solo" part of education and start celebrating being together. Take and share USies whenever possible. Take more photos with MANY people, a group of students, a department planning, or teachers outside at recess playing kickball. You can still use your phone and point it at yourself, just do it with "all of us" to share the moment not only on social media but in live time.

Take A Staff Field Trip: When you have a half day or full day PD, go enjoy something fun; away from the office. Do something in your community that matches your goals. For example, if your focus is social-emotional learning, visit someone in the community who can talk to support you. If you are looking at improving two-way communication, visit a real estate agency or a local business to discuss customer service. Staff productivity and motivation can decay when confined to the school library every time a PD day rolls around. Spending time away from the school with colleagues can be a positively refreshing experience. It can also show staff you value job satisfaction and relevant learning. And maybe sometimes just surprise them and meet at the mini-golf course for an hour of fun. Every hole has a theme for them to talk about, such as the best lesson idea or a great book you read. Having fun as a team can go a long way toward improving morale and maintaining a "together" mindset.

Support Local Restaurants: Think back to a win-win situation. People have to eat, and you want to support local business; why not take a break from the usual staff lunches by visiting a local restaurant for a meeting? Or you can bring a food truck to the office for takeout and an outdoor lunch meeting. These activities are great for your team to eat and socialize, allowing them to recharge and feel valued.

Introducing fun into the workplace, even if it's a school, is an excellent opportunity to shift the way things are done. It can increase staff happiness, productivity, and retention rates. Most importantly, it can improve the overall feelings toward the school, other staff members, and the students.

Pause Moment:

Reflect on the following questions:

- Do I have fun at work?
- What are some activities I have found fun at work?
- What can I do to increase the fun our team has at work?

Conclusion
Stronger Together

None of us is as smart as all of us.
—Ken Blanchard, American Author and Motivational Speaker

When a school develops a collaborative community, it encourages all stakeholders to work together toward shared goals and objectives. This collaborative effort produces faster and more sustainable results with less effort.

Collaboration has a significant, positive impact on:

- Teamwork
- Innovation and creativity
- Reducing teacher turnover
- Sharing talents and knowledge
- A sense of well-being

After reading this book, I recommend reflecting on the content and your current practices to help develop an action plan to shift to or enhance collaboration at your school. School culture is "the way we do things." Your school or classroom culture impacts the immediate environment and what people/students believe and value. Culture is a product of the relationship history in a school. Climate, on the other hand, is how current staff perceive those relationships in the present. Developing a collaborative community will set the tone for culture: "This is important to us as a school."

I am going to leave you all with a challenge. Imagine you are in the elevator and in walks a parent looking at houses in your district. It's a ride with many floors, so you know it's going to be at least 60 seconds. That parent then says to you, "I understand you are a principal/teacher in this school district. Tell me something about your school's culture that you're proud of." The elevator doors close, and it's your turn to speak. What are you going to say? You have 60 seconds. GO!

Share your elevator story with someone at school and with the world on *Twitter* using the hashtag #**StrongerTogether.** Let's all be Stronger Together.

#STRONGERTOGETHER

References

City, E. A. (2011). Learning from instructional rounds. *Educational Leadership, 69*(2), 36-41.

City, E. A., Elmore, R. F., Teitel, L., & Fiarman, S. E. (2009). Instructional rounds in education: A network approach to improving teaching and learning Cambridge, Mass: Harvard Education Press.

Darling-Hammond (2000a). How education matters. *Journal of Teacher Education, 51*(3), 166-173.

Doran G., Miller A., & Cunningham J. (1981) There's a S.M.A.R.T. way to write management goals and objectives, Management Review, Vol. 70, Issue 11, pp. 35-36.

Feeney, E. (2014). Design principles for learning to guide teacher walkthroughs. Clearing House, Vol. 87 Issue 1, p21-29. 9p.

Flores, M. A. (2004). The impact of school culture and leadership on new teachers' learning in the workplace. *International Journal of Leadership in Education, 7*(4), 297-318.

Gac-Artigas , Alejandro (2018) Saving the Education System, Springboard Collaborative, <https://www.springboardcollaborative.org/saving-the-education-system>

Hill, Nancy & Tyson, Diane (2009), Parental Involvement in Middle School: A Meta-Analytic Assessment of the Strategies That Promote Achievement, American Psychological Association, Vol. 45, No. 3, 740–763

Hodges, Tim (2018) School Engagement Is More Than Just Talk, *Education Magazine*, <https://www.gallup.com/education/244022/school-engagement-talk.aspx>

Johnson, S. M., Kraft, M. A., & Papay, J. P. (2012). How context matters in high-need schools: The effects of teachers' working conditions on their professional satisfaction and their students' achievement. *Teachers College Record*, *114*(10), 1-39.

Jove, G. (2011). How do I improve what I am doing as a teacher, teacher educator and action-researcher through reflection? A learning walk from lleida to winchester and back again. *Educational Action Research, 19*(3), 261-278. doi:10.1080/09650792.2011.600526

Kundu, Anindya (2020)The Power of Student Agency: Looking Beyond Grit to Close the Opportunity Gap, Teachers College Press

Lemons, R. W., & Helsing, D. (2009). Learning to walk, walking to learn. *Phi Delta Kappan, 90*(7), 478-484.

Marzano, R. J., Waters, T., & McNulty, B. A. (2005). *School leadership that works : From research to results* Alexandria, Va. : Association for Supervision and Curriculum Development ;

Aurora, Col. : Mid-continent Research for Education and Learning.

Morris, M. (2016) School and District Leadership and the Job Satisfaction of Novice Teachers: The Influence of Distributive Leadership: Boston College Dissertation

Roberts, John E., (2012) *Instructional Rounds in Action*. Cambridge, Mass.: Harvard Education Press, 2012

Roegman, R., & Riehl, C. (2012). Playing Doctor With Education: Considerations in Using Medical Rounds as a Model for Instructional Rounds. *Journal of School Leadership*, *22*(5).

Sousa, David (2015)Engaging the Rewired Brain 1st Edition, Learning Sciences International

Spielberg, Lela (2011) Successful Family Engagement in the Classroom: What teachers need to know and be able to do to engage families in raising student achievement, Flamboyan Foundation

Toshalis, Eric and Nakkula, Michael J. (2012), Motivation, Engagement, and Student Voice, Jobs for the Future

About the Author

Dr. Matthew X. Joseph has been a school and district leader in many capacities in public education over his 28 years in the field. Experiences such as Executive Director of Teaching and Learning, the Director of Curriculum and Instruction, Director of Digital Learning and Innovation, elementary school principal, classroom teacher, and district professional development specialist have provided Matt incredible insights on how to best support teaching and learning and led to nationally published articles and opportunities to speak at multiple state and national events. His master's degree is in special education and his Ed.D. in Educational Leadership from Boston College. He is the author of Stronger Together: The Power of Connections Within a School Community, Power Of Connections: Connecting Educators, Cultivating Professional Learning Networks, & Redefining Educator Collaboration, and co-author of Modern Mentor, Reimagining Mentorship in Education.

Matt is the CEO of X-Factor EDU. X-Factor EDU started in 2016 after he finished his Ed.D in educational leadership from Boston College. He began his journey to supporting educators and districts. X-Factor EDU is a full-service professional development organization with educators from multiple countries and backgrounds. In addition to publishing the voice of amazing educators, we provide leadership coaching, district consulting and workshops, and keynotes around many educational topics.

Matt is the president-elect of MASCD (The Massachusetts chapter of ASCD) and recognized in 2021 as one of 10 national leaders on the rise.

To learn more about Matt or book him for a visit to your school, district, or event visit https://mxjedu.net

About the Editor

Christine Raves-Weinstein currently serves as a high school Assistant Principal in Massachusetts, USA and previously worked as a high school science department chair for four years and classroom teacher for 15. Diagnosed with anxiety and depression at 23, Christine began her journey towards mental wellness. She began a non-profit organization in June of 2017 aimed at removing the stigma of mental illness and promoting physical activity as a means to cope with anxiety.

As an avid writer and educator, Christine became passionate about bridging the two with her advocacy for mental health. Since March of 2019, she has had numerous nationally published articles including the number one most read article of 2019 on *eSchool News* (she also had the number six and eight most read articles in that year). She has also published articles with *District Administration*, the *Teach Better Team*, *Tech & Learning* and *SmartBrief*.

Christine has presented at numerous national conferences including ASCD CEL 2019, Empower20 (selected), ASCD CTE 2020 (selected), the Tech &

Learning 2020 Virtual Leadership Summit, the 2020 ASCD Virtual Conference, ESEA 2021 National Conference, FETC 2022 and has provided professional development for educators in various districts. Christine is an MASCD Board Member, author of the book *Anxious* (Times10, March 2020), *Fighting Your Inner Voice* (Code Breaker, August 2021) and member of the CodeBreaker Leadership Team. Follow her work on Twitter @RavesiWeinstein and on YouTube at http://bit.ly/TheRunnersHigh. For more information about Christine, please visit her website at www.ravesiweinstein.com

CODE BREAKER INC.

Breaking code isn't just about programming, it's about disrupting the status quo. It is about challenging social norms. It is about having critical conversations. It is about challenging systematic beliefs. It is about educating the whole child - mind, body, and soul.

To learn more about

CODE BREAKER INC.

and our services,

visit www.codebreakeredu.com

INSPIRE · INNOVATE

LEAD · TEACH · LEARN

Code BREAKER

Thank you to all our X-Factor partners!
Your efforts will directly support educators' growth and access to resources necessary for improving teaching and learning.
Because of you, we are all Stronger Together.

X FACTOR

Manufactured by Amazon.ca
Bolton, ON

22291981R00094